Advance Praise

"*Destiny's Daughter* is an inspirational book for all ages who have dreams and want to learn how one woman, Dr. Mary Edwards Walker, achieved remarkable results. The book goes beyond the life of Mary Walker and provides the reader with historical insights into our country's political and social challenges that governed people's lives."

— Millie Mack, author

"*Destiny's Daughter* is the story of Dr. Mary Walker, a groundbreaking woman and the only female Medal of Honor recipient. She was definitely a woman who knew what she wanted to do with her life. Some people might call her eccentric, but everyone should call her heroic. Destiny's Daughter shows you why."

— James Rada, author of *Battlefield Angels: The Daughters of Charity Work as Civil War Nurses*

"*Destiny's Daughter* provided many interesting facts about Mary Walker, her family and the time she lived. I liked the incidental background history about the Presidents, other suffragists and notable people included in the narrative. Walker's fight for women's right to dress as they choose is an interesting part of her story but there is so much more to learn about her. Walker's persistence is admirable."

— Mary Hestner, teacher

"Because Mary Walker was a woman, they tried to break her will and destroy her dreams, but she persevered and made important contributions despite the numbskulls she battled along the way. This is an engaging and inspirational biography about a woman who was way ahead of her time."

— Eileen Haavik McIntire, author of the *90s Club* mysteries.

"*Destiny's Daughter* is an interesting and entertaining read about a woman who was ahead of her time. This portrait of Dr. Mary Edwards Walker is not only an account of an extraordinary woman but it also provides insight and encouragement for every young woman who has a vision and the desire beyond the limitations imposed on her by society."

— Karen Pasquale, teacher

Destiny's Daughter

Destiny's Daughter

Highlighting the life of Mary Edwards Walker,
Maverick Suffragist, Doctor,
and Medal of Honor Recipient

An Advocate for Women from Then to Now

Frances Altman

Apprentice
House Press
Loyola University Maryland

First Edition

Library of Congress Control Number: 2022949901

Hardcover ISBN: 978-1-62720-422-4
Paperback ISBN: 978-1-62720-423-1
Ebook ISBN: 978-1-62720-424-8

Design by Grace Noonan
Editorial Development by Sam Dickson
Promotional Development by Brett Duffy

Published by Apprentice House Press

Apprentice
House Press
Loyola University Maryland

Loyola University Maryland
4501 N. Charles Street, Baltimore, MD 21210
410.617.5265
www.ApprenticeHouse.com

info@ApprenticeHouse.com

To Karen, Allison and Hannah

Contents

Foreword

Let me tell you about a woman I met many years ago in the pages of history. Her name was Dr. Mary Edwards Walker. Through the years she taught me many things. Bits and pieces of advice, opinion, vision. At times I remembered to use them. Now I pass along some highlights from her life to you

This book is meant to reframe the view that too often has been given of her. It is an observation of the dynamic life of a woman I discovered in a small clipping in a newspaper. At that time, she happened to be the only woman who had received the Medal of Honor and still is. But that was not why over fifty years ago I began researching her life, actions and writings.

At the time I had previously written four children's biographies for the publisher, T.S. Dennison. I thought Mary would make a good story for another. To prove my point, I sold an article about her to the *Dayton Leisure*. Unfortunately, my publisher closed and I moved on to develop a career in public relations and marketing.

Along the way I met , Mercedes Graf, at Elmhurst College, in Illinois met Mercedes Graf at Elmhurst College in .Illinois. She had written two small books about Mary Walker. She, too, had found Mary's comments to be encouraging, and gave me a copy of Mary's book, "*Hit.*"

But for the most part, Mary's manuscript remained in my file. From time to time I would get is out, rewriting it from different viewpoints. I did more research. I made inquiries; I visited historical sources. My curiosity continued.

Often, I found a few of her comments to be encouraging, or her philosophy similar to mine. Most of all, I admired her ability to look ahead positively, to always have a survival plan, to be able to reinvent herself and be resilient.

It may have been a coincidence that, when downsized from a corporation, I used her advice. It worked. It moved me on.

So here we are in a Pandemic era. Now I know the feel to be eighty, as was Mary was when she retired. I move slowly too, and walk with a cane, as did she. Wondrously, research now is only finger tips away as many historical files are digital. And so, I welcomed Mary Edwards Walker back into my writing life at a dreary time. Completing her story, as I saw it, became a mission.

I acknowledge she practiced many of the principles I borrowed and used. Perhaps young women today may be in need of similar advice. For instance, she urged us to *wear sturdy shoes* if we are going to rally, march, or stand in a line. That sometimes it might be better to *hold your tongue* or *listen*. Make it a habit to *keep learning*, to *plan ahead*, to *be curious* and *value your worth*. Most of all: *be resilient*.

Indeed, one day Destiny may send forth another Daughter such as Mary Walker. May she find success.

—Frances Altman

Chapter 1

The Beginning

Mary Edwards Walker was a feisty, petite girl who loved to jump, run like a deer, and kick at rocks in the dirt as she walked along the Bunker Hill Road near her home. When no one was watching she was likely to pull up a handful of dandelions, blow their puffy tops away, and then nibble at the leaves, providing they were tender. She loved being out in the open air, playing pretend, or following her father around to watch him tinker with farm machinery.

Teasing her four older sisters provided a good pastime too, laughing when they screeched and shooed her away. They were the Walker children. There were six of them—Vesta, the oldest, then Aurora Borealis who was Mary's self-appointed protector, Luna, and Cynthia. Then there was their baby brother, Alvah Jr. who was four years younger than Mary. Watching, rocking, and feeding him were full time chores. Everyone had a job in the Walker family, and caring for her brother was Mary's.

The Walkers had migrated from Greenwich, Massachusetts, traveling by springboard wagon to settle in Syracuse, New York. Four children had been born at that time —four girls and a boy, named Abel, who died when only a few days old. The family then moved further west, settling on a 33-acre farm located on Bunker Hill Road, south of the town of Oswego. Mary and Alvah Jr. were born after the family settled down there. Mary was born on November 25, 1832.

Growing up in the Walker family was considerably different than in most families of the time.

There was always so much going on. There were the older sisters , loving but bossy, often taking on the role of a mother.

"Brush your hair thirty strokes."

"Pull your socks up." Or "wash your hands."

Mary's father, Alvah Senior was an easy-going carpenter, handyman and teacher who, due to his own health problems, had a strong interest in studying the effects of medicines, minerals, and herbs. Because of his deep interest in healing preparations and herbs, many people mistook him for a doctor and often called on him for healing remedies.

He also loved to teach, so much so that together with his wife, Vesta Whitcomb Walker, they built and started the first "free school" in that region of New York State. They both taught there. They also invited and welcomed many travelers to drop in at their two-story home and stay awhile, pitching in to work for their room and board and becoming part of an extended family.

Mary's mother, Vesta Walker, was a veteran teacher, who had begun home schooling her daughters at an early age. As soon as the older girls reached the ages of thirteen or fourteen, they joined their mother in teaching in the family-run school.

"We can help you gather flowers," Mary often may have volunteered that she and her brother could help out in this way.

One of the things that Mrs. Walker liked to do was to

brighten her classroom with vases of cut flowers. Some had been grown in the family's garden, and others were wildflowers that grew in the fields around them. Brightening her classroom in this manner gained her a small reputation among those who knew her in the community.

Both of Mary's parents were the children of sturdy Massachusetts settlers who in the early years of their marriage, decided to slowly move westward. Alvah (1798-1880) was the son of Abel Walker (1770-1718) and his wife, Mary Snow. Mary Walker may have been named after her grandmother; a pattern established in the family of naming children after earlier relatives.

Although Alvah had been educated as a teacher and healer, over time he drifted away from practicing medicine and into teaching and managing the family's farm. Sometimes the neighbors may have seen more of Mary's father than his family did because he had built a reputation as a great neighbor who was a man always ready and willing to help just about everyone. He also was recognized as a strong abolitionist.

A strong farm family

The Walkers did not consider themselves as poor because other families had even less. Sometimes, Alvah would barter or trade for services, but generally he followed his motto of "helping one another" without payment. In addition to teaching, they followed the traditional seasonal farming patterns of plowing, planting, and harvesting. Throughout the summer and fall there was weeding to be done and the harvesting of vegetables such as tomatoes, beans, peas, corn, and later squash and potatoes.

Canning or drying the vegetables, and later in the Fall

picking apples, meant being able to survive. Feeding such a large family over the winter months when heavy snow covered the farm land was not an easy task. In between, they gathered nuts and herbs, adding this to the regular family chores of doing laundry, ironing, house cleaning, and sewing.

"Monday is for washing. Tuesday is for ironing," went a song children often sang.

Their hometown, Oswego, was located in north central New York State on the banks of Lake Ontario. Winters were generally fierce, with chill winds blowing off the Lake, deep snow, and near blizzard conditions. But winters could be fun too. Snowball fights, sledding, and building snow forts and snowmen were typical outdoor activities. Along with play went shoveling paths as walkways from the house to the barn and other out-buildings.

Farm folks had to be tough and resilient, bundling up in layers of clothes from long underwear to heavy coats. Their time spent indoors was devoted to studies or sewing lessons and cooking.

Absorbing a philosophy

It was the Walker family's philosophy that sharing the farm work and chores made them strong, and prepared them for the next chapter in their lives.

The women adopted the kind of clothing that would be comfortable as they performed their work, taking to wearing pants underneath their dresses. Pants protected their legs from morning dew or dust, snow or rain. The Walkers may have adopted this dress code from the Oneida Community women who lived in a communal residence in Oneida, New York, and whose skirts were hemmed about twelve inches above their pants.

Over time, Alvah Walker became a popular neighbor among the area's citizens. He enjoyed this casual way of life, and found it particularly easy to take on some of the philosophies of the abolitionists and politicians that rallied around the countryside.

He was an avid reader, even of foreign publications, and particularly liked reading about health and medical topics. He followed the Methodist doctrine, attending meetings regularly and writing brief descriptions every day in his journal. As a side vocation he tanned small animal hides, using these cured materials to make ladies boots and gloves that he sold readily to customers around Oswego.

Observers might have said Mary idolized her father. She'd observe many of his activities, sometimes helping a little or just watching her father at work. She saw that he listened to people, and began to train herself to listen as well.

Before she was a dozen years old Mary was familiar with many medicinal remedies of the day such as making horehound soup and crystallizing it into cough drops. Other favorites of the time included drinking herb tea, and the use of calomel and camphor oil for chest ailments.

A corner of almost every farm garden included a plot devoted to herbs, eaten fresh or dried. Rosemary, sage, thyme and chives were commonly used in cooking. Medicinal herbs such as mint and wintergreen helped sooth rough throats and were also used for seasonings and teas. Mint was versatile and popular for upset stomachs and bowel problems; wild mustard was gathered and crushed for use as a chest poultice; and dandelions were prescribed as a remedy for liver ailments. In the spring tender dock, mustard and dandelion greens were picked for salads or stewing.

In keeping with the times, most farmers kept a wide variety of these home-grown medicines around and used them to treat both human and animal illnesses.

In addition to the Walker family, there were continually students, patients and live-ins coming and going from the farm.

"Remember to call the gentlemen visitors "mister" often reminded Vesta Walker. These visitors brought news and interesting stories to the Walker family.

• • •

This was the environment in which Mary Walker thrived.

Mary's attention may first have been directed to care giving by an appeal from a local missionary. He had urged the young women of the community to take up nursing older or poor women, as many of them did not have access to male physicians..

"Go ahead, learn all you can," urged her father. He had learned all of his health information by reading books and treating neighbors and friends.

It wasn't long before Mary was sitting up with individuals who were ill and observing their symptoms. She no doubt gave them some of the common home prescribed remedies of the day. All kinds of medical information interested her, including the review of coroner's reports.

Eventually Mary got up the courage to approach their family doctor.

"May I borrow one of your medical books," she asked. He thought she was just curious, and loaned it to her more as a joke. Then he dismissed her interest by calling it "a childish whim. It will soon go away," but it didn't. She hid away in her room continuing to read medical books.

"You'll make a wonderful nurse," people outside the family told Mary. Secretly she told herself over and over: "I want to be a doctor."

Chapter 2

A Family of Freethinkers

Growing up in this environment not only inspired, but bolstered Mary's determination to become a doctor. She never said exactly when she made that definite decision, but she did recognize the fact that she enjoyed care giving and that her curious mind continued to want to learn more.

Mary's interests in nursing were nurtured by both of her parents, but more particularly by her father, who believed she had an aptitude for working with the sick. He directed her attention to ancient Egypt, where the medical profession was almost entirely in the hands of women; there were hardly any diseases there at all, particularly children's' diseases. Mary occassionally considered becoming a missionary, but was always quick to dismiss that idea.

Mary's mother, Vesta, was a little more serious and sterner than her husband, but they made an ideal couple. She was a "Massachusetts Whitcomb" closely related to a Reverend James Whitcomb, who was a relative of the poet James Whitcomb Riley. They traced their ancestry back to the signers of the Mayflower Pact and the stalwart "Widow Walker" of Plymouth Colony. By becoming a teacher, Vesta had followed in the footsteps of her mother, Polly Hinds. During that era teaching was about the only professional occupation available to women, and Vesta had been able to establish a modest reputation of her own.

Considering the value the Walkers placed on education, it was not surprising that they decided to even mortgage the family farm to continue educating their daughters at Falley Seminary in nearby Fulton, New York. It had a good Methodist background and eventually all of the Walker children boarded at the school at one time or another.

Having been home schooled by her parents, Mary's education was well advanced, so much so that she qualified to accept a teaching position while still a teenager. During the year of 1848, at age sixteen she began teaching at Falley's while continuing to attend classes there. Among her favorite topics were anatomy, a prescribed study, and current world events.

Turbulent times

Politics would have been difficult for the Walker family to ignore, especially in New York State.

During the years when Mary was teaching there were three political parties: the Whigs, Democrats and Republicans. One man, prominent at the time in New York politics, was Millard Fillmore from Buffalo. He served eight years in the House of Representatives and was elected Vice President. During those days fierce debates took place about what was called the Compromise of 1850.

In July 1850 President Zachery Taylor died and Fillmore became President.

New Yorkers were proud of their favorite son. But Fillmore was not reelected. He opposed the up-and-coming Abraham Lincoln and the philosophies of a Reconstruction plan that was growing.

Seneca Falls

At that time anyone who followed the American abolitionist movement would have been interested in a special conference that was held at Seneca Falls, New York. The conference was the collaboration of Elizabeth Cody Stanton and Lucrelia Mott, both activists in the movement to abolish slavery, as well as supporting women's rights. It drew up to three hundred men and women in attendance.

Mary later read about this conference, absorbing what had happened there and following its outcome.

Stanton and Mott happened to have met for the first time a couple of years earlier in London, when they had been appointed to attend the World Anti-Slavery Conference. However, upon arrival they learned that the conference was not open to women so they were not permitted to participate. But they kept in touch upon their return to America and decided to put their own conference together.

One of the outcomes of their Conference was the writing of the Declaration of Sentiment of the Seneca Falls Convention, using the model of the U.S. Declaration of Independence. It demanded that the rights of women as right-bearing individuals be acknowledged and respected by society. It was signed by sixty-eight women and thirty-two men.

Elizabeth Cody Stanton went on continuing to promote her convictions. She wrote what she called a *Women's Bible*. She denounced the clergy for not upholding women's rights and seemed to have little trouble finding pulpits from which to talk. To many listeners, her religious convictions did not seem so strong.

As a teenager, Mary was always out and about doing something with her family. Already labeled as abolitionists by their neighbors, she particularly relished when her father would hitch up the team to the springboard wagon, and load it with blankets and food. That meant they were going to head into town or another nearby area of the State to watch or even march or protest in parades. The cause never seemed to matter.

The Walker family shared many viewpoints. Definitely, they favored women's rights; on other days other issues. On the weekends they were among those families who would go down to the rallies on the levee, stay all day and maybe camp out along the river banks when night came. Mary enthusiastically participated in such rallies keeping pace with both the marchers and the music.

Minstrels, many coming from New York City, would follow the crowds and join in with the rallies to keep everyone entertained. Some were black musicians and performers, others white musicians with burnt cork smeared over their faces. Their lively tunes kept the crowds alive and awake long into the night with loud singing and stomping feet.

As the months passed the rallies increased, growing in size as rumors grew of the possibility of a war between certain northern and southern states. Along the river banks and lake shore, bonfires would light up the night sky and offer an eerie glow all around. A charred aroma came from the crackling burning timbers. There, the Walker family would gather with their neighbors or other freethinkers and listen to the different speeches delivered by crusaders, traveling evangelists, and politicians.

Notably, the minstrels' music coincided with the abolitionist movement in places like New York City and the Bowery. Then small troupes of two and three musicians would circulate all over the region from New York to Washington City and helped popularize a variety of Northern and Southern hymns from the churches there. Livelier plantation songs were sung to banjo and fiddle twangs. Dancing of all types took place, from vivacious stomping feet to variations of shuffling and Irish jigging.

To most of the people gathered, the blackface singer represented the enslaved people of the South. The singers gave a happy impression while tambourines expressed a gypsy lifestyle. Their performances were not representative of plantation life.

> *"Camp town ladies sing this song,*
> *Doo-dah! Doo-dah!*
> *Camp town racetrack just five miles long,*
> *Oh, Doo-dah Day!"*

Their songs were old and simple so that both adults and children joined in singing together. They were quick and easily learned tunes that could be remembered by heart and then be sung when back home.

Gradually as the night grew on, more spirited songs like "Old Dan Tucker" and new songs like "Oh! Susanna" would be replaced with hymns such as "Glory, Glory Hallelujah!"

All the while Mary was forming many of the independent characteristics and strong determinations that she would exhibit throughout her lifetime. Confidence, curiosity, patience, resilience, perseverance and courage—all were becoming visible within her personality. Most of all she was steadfastly persistent as she persevered in what she believed to be the right course for her.

"I will be a doctor. I will," she vowed.

Chapter 3

Determination

"You can be anything you want to be," her father and mother promised. "We will help you all we can."

There was no doubt that Mary was a spirited young woman; only a step away from being a grown up, and absorbing every moment of it. She was a feisty contradiction in the way she was beginning to dress, sometimes more like a tomboy than a proper young lady.

At five feet tall she was petite, slender, and according to some, attractive. Her hair hung long and soft, falling to her waist. On special occasions, she would wear her hair in long tight curls, the kind that were usually shaped with a hot iron or rag curlers. But much of the time she just let her hair stay short and it curled by itself.

She was pretty, her sisters told her.

"Pretty is as pretty does," they also teased her.

She was always thoughtful. Her smile may not have come often or readily, but her eyes made up for it with a friendly sparkle. They were always touched with a hint of mischief that pointed to a keen, free-spirited disposition. She was smart and able to articulate well. Some people even described her as sweet.

In later years, this special combination of wistful youth,

ability, and determination created a natural charm. When coupled with her petite size, men tended to treat her protectively without knowing why. They'd admire her ability to talk with them in a comfortable and informal manner on almost any topic; a gift she had inherited from her father.

Most of all Mary loved abandoning the customary garments prescribed for women to wear. She and her sisters had tried all of them. Crinoline petticoats hidden under long falling starched skirts were popular for gala dances. The layers of those crinoline petti- coats hung heavily from the waist. Mary rejected them. She also tried wearing the pantaloons style pants, patterned after Turkish cut leggings, and then "bloomers," a bifurcated skirt designed by Mrs. Elizabeth Smith Miller.

Bloomers actually took its name from the pages of *Lily* magazine where it was highly publicized by its Iowa publisher, Amelia Jenks Bloomer. The publication was distributed to about 6,000 readers. Bloomer had started her magazine in 1849 to primarily promote women's' rights, temperance, and comfortable clothing that did not bind a women's body.

Even a song was written about the style that was often chanted across the country:

> *Heigh, Ho, in rain or snow*
> *Bloomers now are all the go.*
> *Twenty tailors take the stitches.*
> *Twenty women wear the breeches,*
> *Heigh, Ho, in rain or snow.*

> *One store advertisement called them*
> *"trouserettes."*

Go Bloomerettes!

The original Bloomer costume reached down to the ankles and was accompanied by a short skirt that came to about the knees. The skirt appeared longer than most on women of Mary's height – about five feet.

Amelia Bloomer's promotion in *Lily* of what she considered a sensible style of dressing for the most "sensible woman" spanned a period of about six years. It earned her and her publication notoriety and inspired other feminists to wear them and write about them. Parades of protesting women wearing bloomers were held in many towns. One widely read author of note was Louisa May Alcott, who likewise dreamed of creating "sensible women" in articles and in her books for women.

But to Mary, pants like the boys wore were easier to pull on and wear. Mary loved kicking her legs free and being comfortable when she walked or marched.

A straight-leg tailored style was what she liked best. It was not long before Mary started wearing this style of pants under her short dresses all the time. They suited her free spirit. Sometimes she would choose to just wear a man's shirt, jacket or vest with them instead of a dress or a skirt. Most times she wore suspenders to keep them up.

"Throw those long skirts away," urged her parents, who made fun of the fashionable Bloomer pantaloons frequently being worn by women marching at the rallies. They strongly criticized the long skirts for dragging the floor or street and sweeping up dust. Even worse, the skirt often caught on cigar butts, soaked up spilled water or beer, and generally swept the floor.

The Walker women required practical clothing. Cutting the length of the skirt to fit their height gave them freedom for bending over as they worked in the garden, or from stepping on the hem when climbing stairs or standing on a ladder.

"Wear what you like and feel comfortable," said their father over and over. This advice indeed went against the traditional clothing style deemed acceptable for women, but it was the solution that best suited Mary Walker's lifestyle. She held absolutely no qualms at kicking a little dust on tradition.

She also began to design and wear her own version of hygienic underwear, which she was constantly altering for comfort. She called it a "reformed under suit," but it looked something like a man's "long johns."

"It's rape proof," she confided to other women.

As time went on, she made the under suit of linen with a high neck, a loose waist and whole drawers. The long sleeves had wrist bands and the back of the blouse had buttons that kept the rear of the pants closed. Although linen was the most practical fabric, it could be made of silk or a heavier jersey cloth. The legs of the drawers were folded over the ankles' long stockings and then adjusted up over the top buttons of the suit.

Mary was quick to point out that "This not only keeps the ankles warm, but keeps the stockings in place without garters or elastic bands that might cut off the circulation or contribute to varicose veins."

Forming an opinion

Nurtured by the philosophy and teachings of her parents, rally speakers, and the growing influence of women's activists , Mary Walker grew up accepting their principles, while also forming her own. Newspapers were quick to quote from the lectures of Lucretia Mott and Elizabeth Cady Stanton. Other women were also beginning to join those talking about the new philosophies that, additionally, included condemning smoking and alcohol.

"I want to study all I can about medicine," Mary told her friends and fellow students at Falley's. She received only snickers and criticism in return. But for financial reasons she stuck it out, carefully putting her earnings away toward the day when she knew she would be able to attend a medical institution.

At age twenty, Mary moved on to teach at a school in Minetto, New York. She again made the mistake of telling a few students and friends that she intended to study medicine.

She started encountering opposition, particularly from the young men who made up the majority of the student body. By the end of her first-year, she had made up her mind that "teaching isn't for me any longer." She missed her family and their support. Her desire to become a doctor had grown stronger than ever.

It was 1852 and some changes were slowly taking place.

Mary had tried to keep track of what was happening to the few women who were trying to break the barrier and become doctors in America, as well as in Europe. Elizabeth Blackwell had received her medical degree in 1849 from the Geneva College of Medicine, making her the first female medical doctor in America. The newspapers called it a "landmark."

"It says other medical schools are going to review their policies. I'm going to apply to all of them," announced Mary.

Mary learned that Elizabeth Blackwell's sister, Emily Blackwell, was also attending medical school. This fact reinforced Mary's determination. She envisioned walking in their footsteps. But the medical colleges held to their policies; no women.

That did not stop Mary. As weeks turned into months,

she began applying to the medical schools near Oswego. She applied twice to nearby Syracuse Medical College. She even considered writing them using just her initials so they would not know she was a woman.

Daily, Mary was demonstrating that she was becoming a determined and prolific letter writer.

Finally, a response

At last, it happened. Mary's application was accepted!

The Syracuse Medical College was among America's first medical schools that instated the unique philosophy of accepting men and women on an equal basis. Mary's unconventional attitude seemed to mesh with the school's eclectic reputation. A student could earn a medical degree by completing three thirteen-week semesters of medical training.

Mary's parents were as excited as she, and willing to pay fifty-five dollars for each semester. In later months, other women were accepted, but Mary had the distinction of being the only woman in her medical class.

"At last, it's happening." Mary was overwhelmed with excitement. "It's happening!" she kept saying and singing it over and over to herself. At last, her dream was coming true.

Chapter 4

A Doctor at Last!

Mary's life at Syracuse Medical College changed drastically from her quiet life on the farm. She enthusiastically threw herself into her studies. Here, again, she met opposition from students who criticized her ambition to become a doctor. But not from everyone.

One young man in particular captured her interest. His name was Albert Y. Miller. Also studying to become a doctor, his interests were similar to Mary's. He admired her perseverance, her spirit. The two soon developed a close relationship. Mary described it as a romantic chemistry that existed between them. She had never felt exactly that way.

He demonstrated all the attributes of someone she could trust and bond with. Before she knew it, Mary was confiding privately to friends that she felt she was falling deeply in love with Albert Miller!

Doctor Mary Walker

Mary loved saying it over and over, listening to the sounds roll off her tongue.

"Mary is a doctor. A doctor! Doctor Mary Edwards Walker." She was anxious to move on.

Armed with her new credentials proclaiming her a medical

physician, "Doctor Mary Walker" went back to her home town of Oswego, hopeful that she could begin practicing there.

Bursting with enthusiasm she called on doctors she had known her entire life. Some of them had even loaned her a medical journal or two, or talked to her upon occasion about joining their profession; but even the doctors who had encouraged her to sit up with sick patients and considered her to have been reliable, turned her away. They adamantly refused to even consider her as a medical partner.

"No one will come to a woman doctor," they told her.

Undaunted, Mary traveled to Columbus, Ohio, where she had relatives, and attempted to set up an office there. Setting up a medical practice primarily entailed hanging up your physician's sign or "shingle" outside your residence or office.

Mary's existence in Ohio lasted only a few months before she returned home in a state of dejection. She was totally surprised at the public's reaction to women physicians. Women had always been recognized as caregivers, so why not doctors?

"We've never seen you so discouraged?" Her family and friends rallied around her, offering suggestions as to what she might do next.

"I am discouraged," Mary admitted, "but not defeated!" She turned to confide in Aurora, her oldest sister and benefactor. Aurora had married a prosperous man. She strongly believed in Mary's efforts and promised to help her.

"It might be all right for a woman to want to be a nurse, but not a doctor," appeared to be the sentiment.

People weren't ready to accept women in that position either, although it was starting to catch on.

Those patients who had knocked on Dr. Mary Walker's door in Ohio were far and few between and often were too poor to pay. She ended up treating many of them for free or in exchange for a homemade pie or a freshly baked loaf of bread.

"A woman doctor? Absolutely not! Not even for a sick child!" And certainly not for a man either, it seemed.

Even Mary's role model, Elizabeth Blackwell, had met this same resistance. She had been forced to leave her school and go to England to find a real position as a doctor.

Mary is in love

In the meantime, only a few hundred miles away, Mary's boyfriend, or as some said, possibly her fiancé, Albert Miller, was busily setting up his practice in Rome, New York. Rumor had it he was doing very well for himself.

To family and close friends who knew Mary and Albert, it didn't make a lot of sense that "those two kids should be living apart, one doing well and the other not." During the summer, Mary and Albert continued courting until their serious romance ended in a proposal of marriage.

"Let's get married now." Then Mary could accompany Albert back to Rome not only as his wife, but as his new partner.

Yes, Mary loved Albert very deeply. They had been sexually attracted to one another from their first days after meeting in medical school. Mary was a romantic at heart, and her love for Albert held a special meaning to her. She described it as "a feeling lying just beneath her skin." It was such a strong emotion between the two that she compared it to a magnetic cable connecting them.

But Mary also held very strong beliefs on woman's rights, feminine hygiene, and dress reform. From childhood, she had been told she could be anything she wanted to be. She already considered herself to be free and able to go wherever and do whatever she pleased. However, she had not exhibited it very much throughout the year in medical school.

Right from the beginning of their renewed relationship, Mary began to occasionally exasperate her future husband. For example, Mary's choice of a wedding costume could not have come as a surprise to Albert. A skirt worn over pants had become her favorite combination and she had experimented with several styles of her"Reform Dress" while they were together in school. Maybe he thought it was a whim that would go away or something she was just talking about. But she also liked pants with a jacket or combinations of both.

Albert protested, but Mary persisted that she would wear her reform dress for their wedding. Then she insisted on rewriting their wedding vows, taking out the word "obey," which in those days was a sacrament of the traditional wedding ceremony. She had read somewhere that the activist Lucretia Mott had taken "obey" out of her ceremony. Another sticky point was that even though Mary had been brought up as a Methodist, for some unknown reason she insisted that the ceremony be performed by a Unitarian minister.

Never the less it turned out to be a joyful day with many good wishes from family and friends who gathered at the Walker home for the wedding.

Immediately following the wedding, the couple returned to Rome to spend their honeymoon. And, begin working together to build their practice.

One can only speculate as to what may have happened in the following months. Mary never confided to anyone, including her sisters. But it was a time that brought both happy and hectic tears, as Mary threw herself into creating a new lifestyle.

Surprise! What could happen next?

As soon as the newly-weds reached Rome. Mary began using the name "Dr. Mary E. Miller Walker" or variations of it, signing prescriptions and other letters using that name. Another of Mary's requests, that grew into demands, was for Albert not to treat women patients. Although Mary had originally considered treating only women and children, she began treating men too. This competitive situation sparked many quarrels between them. Albert insisted that Mary stop treating men. However, he refused to discontinue treating women and children. By then they were continually fussing and acting like spoiled children toward each other.

Perhaps Mary and Albert had never thought ahead to how married life might be or discussed this aspect of their partnership. Or perhaps it became a competitive game between them. Mary had grown up competing with her sisters and brother. She was permitted to express her opinions adamantly. Perhaps her independent spirit wouldn't allow her to reconcile to Albert's wishes. Maybe she really didn't even know how to rescue her marriage that was rapidly turning into shambles.

On the other hand, Albert didn't want to be embarrassed before his new circle of friends and patients. He had come there a year earlier and built a certain reputation. One can only speculate as to what happened in the next few months.

In addition to her practice, Mary kept lecturing about dress reform. There were women's groups throughout New York that favored dress reform, and Mary traveled to speak to them. She was something of a curiosity because she dared to dress in pants daily. The fact that she was also one of the first female physicians practicing in America added an increased interest.

It also became more and more difficult for Albert to explain to his friends why his wife chose to dress in pants or to forgo wifely duties to travel the countryside giving lectures. In fact, many of his friends did not want their wives to learn or discuss intimate subjects such as bathing and pregnancy. Sex in general was a taboo topic

The final blow came when Mary learned that Albert was paying a great deal of attention to other women outside their home and practice. Although she tried to ignore his womanizing—it was becoming obvious that the marriage was spiraling downward into failure. Mary did make inquiries about getting a divorce but learned that grounds for divorce were restrictive in New York State.

Well, that's it!

At last, in late 1859 after one of their quarrels, Albert announced "that's it," and closed his part of the partnership. One day, while Mary was out lecturing, he dismissed the house keeper, boxed up his library and equipment, closed his medical bag and left the town of Rome and his wife behind. He had decided to go on the lecture circuit himself.

Nevertheless, Mary liked the area very much. She lingered in Rome, keeping her small practice going, advocating social issues through local talks. Now she even found the time to help organize a group called the National Dress Reform Association.

Whenever Mary Walker took on a new interest, she had a tendency to throw herself into it, body and soul. She was also embarrassed her husband left her; she needed this preoccupation. She could write letters to prospective members; she could help organize their program. Her strong interest helped her get elected as the Association's vice president.

This was an organization that matched her interests. She promised herself that someday she would become its president. She also started spending her time writing articles for a small magazine called *The Sibyl*. It was a little reform magazine edited and published by Dr. Lydia Saver Hasbrouck of Middletown, New York. Many of the other reform members wrote for the publication as well, so once again Mary's competitive spirit began to push her along.

By this time, Mary had to be in some degree of recovery from her marriage experience. However, in the end, she realized she had fallen short of her expectations for establishing a happy marriage and successful practice. Several of her friends and acquaintances already had established medical practices, alongside successful marriages. Yes, she felt terribly hurt, but most of all embarrassed.

Reflection

Mary also began to reflect a little bit on different phases of her marriage, even as short as it had been. Was it possible that she had become so overwhelmed with the romantic aspects of it all that she had daydreamed too much of how it should be, rather than how their relationship really was? Had she reacted too dramatically? Sometimes she did that. Yet, their friends and family had seen them as a perfect couple. They had nudged and encouraged them to marry.

It had all been so exciting in the beginning, and then reality had begun. Mary wondered if that should be a topic to further explore for a lecture. This was not uncommon in many families. Once married, a woman was considered to be tied to an unhappy and miserable situation for the rest of her life.

One option left to her was to pack up and move back home, where she could begin teaching again and working with her parents on the farm. By this time her sisters had married and lived in nearby communities. However, they were embarrassed by her reform dress and had told her so. Only her oldest sister, Aurora, still stood by her.

"Going home will be tough," Mary admitted to herself. The close marital relationship of her parents was sure to be a constant reminder of her own failed marriage. At that point, Mary may have then let her emotions get the better of her. Impulsively, she confided with Judge House, an old family friend from Oswego, who had relocated to Delhi, Iowa. They decided that it would be better if Mary moved to Delhi, establish a year's residence and file for a divorce in Iowa.

Again, Mary was becoming restless. While waiting those months in Delhi, she contemplated enrolling in Bowen Collegiate Institute, a small college located in the nearby town of Hopkinton. She had heard they taught German, a language she thought she might like to learn. But, she had no more than enrolled, when she became embroiled in an argument with the school's administration over seeking membership in the men's debating society. The Institute asked her to leave and she complied.

Before the year was out, Mary began packing her bags again. She knew now that she needed to move on to the next chapter of her life—whatever that might be. Further disappointment came in learning that she could not obtain a divorce in the State of Iowa either. Her circumstances didn't qualify.

Mary now believed she was ready to seek out other opportunities. Becoming a small-town doctor was out. She had seen a few country doctors driving their one-horse buggies out to care for farmers or sharecroppers. That no longer appealed to her. She had been thinking and reading and reacting logically, and now was feeling like her old self again.

It seemed obvious from reports in the newspapers that the country was seriously approaching a war. That could only mean that medical opportunities would soon be available.

Mary went back to Rome, closed her medical practice and collected whatever belongings she had left there. She decided to go home and wait.

Chapter 5

Hopes and Dreams

Returning to Oswego was definitely the next step. Once back on the farm she began to train herself to endure hardships. What might she encounter in a hostile war environment? She started out by sleeping on the hard wooden floor of her bedroom.

She also consoled herself by remembering that her role model, Dr. Elizabeth Blackwell, also had trouble establishing an American practice, and gone to England.

Mary began making inquiries into what her other opportunities might be. It looked more and more promising that the government medical system offered possibilities. Vesta and Alvah Walker strongly approved of their daughter's decision to seek a medical position within the government. They were willing to advance her travel expenses to travel to Washington City and learn more.

By that time, Mary was restless to be included in the war effort. She was convinced a position with the Union Army seemed most suited to her training. She was becoming more determined than ever to be recognized as a doctor. When she had graduated from Syracuse, she had been told that she was the second woman doctor in the United States; she had wanted to prove herself worthy of that designation. Now, she felt time was passing her by. It was necessary that she renew her determination to keep her eyes on her goal. If she had to go in through the back door—so be it!

Mary Walker was beginning to recognize her own value.

A letter campaign

By now, Mary had become a prolific letter writer. Letters were the customary way of contacting people, but it took many days, even weeks, before a reply would come. That did not discourage her. She did not hesitate to write anyone she heard about or read about in the newspapers, including the President of the United States—Abraham Lincoln.

In her application letter to President Abraham Lincoln, Mary dramatically wrote that she would be willing to be assigned to a female ward, but she would "Much prefer to have an extra surgeon's commission with orders to go whenever and wherever there is a battle," She promised, "I will not shrink from shot and shells." She went on to write that her "life was of no value—if by its loss the interest of future generations shall be promoted."

As the prospects of war continued to dominate the newspaper pages, it was becoming obvious that doctors would be in great demand. War was imminent, they predicted, only weeks away.

Mary mailed off another barrage of letters. She applied in her own name and just as often used only her initials. One was to the Surgeon General of the United States. She repeatedly wrote letters to political names she came across. Still, she was rejected. She hid her tears. Rejection stung, but tenacity and perseverance made up a strong part of her character. She continued writing.

It was also a time when Mary could catch up with what some of her friends were doing. Several of them had married and had children or established some form of practice. She may have been consoled somewhat in news that women physicians were becoming more common, but for the most part they still weren't widely accepted by male doctors or patients.

War begins

Just as predicted, war began. On April 12, 1861, Confederate cannons opened fire on Fort Sumter, the Union Army garrison built in Charleston Harbour. At 2:30 p.m. on April 13, the Commander of the Fort surrendered.

This was the opening battle of the American War Between the states. The following day, the newspapers reported that President Abraham Lincoln had called for 73,000 soldiers to be recruited. A week after the attack on Fort Sumter, the President called a Washington medical administrator named Dorothea Dix, asking if she could set up a nursing system for him.

Lincoln knew Dix and her husband, and was aware of her experience as an administrator in the medical health arena. Dix immediately accepted and was officially named Superintendent of Army Nurses, a volunteer position which she would hold for the next four years.

Mrs. Dix was fifty-nine years old and had already proven herself as a capable organizer of medical affairs. Since about 1841, she had been crusading for reform in the mental health field, assisting in hospitals and prisons where many mentally ill patients often landed when other medical facilities were unavailable. Through her efforts, some progress had been made to correct these problems, but the war made it obvious that battle injuries must take precedent.

Mrs. Dix took her new position seriously. She immediately rolled up her sleeves and began recruiting and selecting women to be trained as nurses.

Mary liked everything she read about Mrs. Dix. Should she write her too? Mary read how colleagues described Mrs. Dix as stern and brusque, a serious, no-nonsense woman who knew the horrors of sickness. Up to this time, military nurses had all been men. Now, because she believed women were better suited as nurses, Mrs. Dix was proposing to train volunteer women to be nurses for the war effort. They would all be over the age of thirty and wear a similar plain, brown uniform. They should be plain looking and wear no jewelry. Mrs. Dix was making it clear to everyone that she was not interested in promoting war romances, nor adventuresses.

While Mrs. Dix was putting her plans in place, Mary decided to write her a letter to request an interview. Mrs. Dix's new hospital project, now called Women's Central Association, strongly appealed to her. But the longer Mary waited to hear from anyone, the more impatient she became. She was already a licensed doctor, although she acknowledged that her practicing of the profession was limited.

She desperately wanted to learn more about the Women's Central Association. She reasoned that once she achieved an interview with Mrs. Dix, she could convince her that women physicians would fit well in her system too. However, she was willing to travel at her own expense to learn more about Dix's plans and hopefully be interviewed.

Time moves slowly

During that same year another woman, by the name of Anna

Carroll, began to make news. She was the daughter of a former Maryland governor, Thomas Carroll, and was familiar with the political activities around Washington. She had written a pamphlet called "The War Powers of the Government," explaining President Abraham Lincoln's legal actions for sending military forces to fight against the Confederacy.

The President liked her writings so much that he referred the pamphlet to Congress and, eventually, ten thousand copies were printed for public distribution. Undoubtedly, Mary, who was becoming an ardent Lincoln admirer, probably read Carroll's pamphlet. Mary liked the way it was presented. Maybe she would try doing that someday with one of her opinion articles.

Precious days passed. Nothing was developing. Mary continued to grow impatient, hearing nothing back from either the President, nor the Surgeon General, and not even Mrs. Dix. She continued preparing herself for facing any hardships or other miserable conditions.

Mary admitted to herself that her practice of medicine had been limited, but she was already a licensed doctor. She was confused. She was frustrated. She was tired of waiting to hear something. It seemed that at every turn the prospects of a woman doctor getting to practice were dismal.

Still, Mary waited; helping the family on the farm, nursing those who came there, and continuing to teach. In other words: doing her share. The days passed slowly, but her hope continued. She wrote more letters. She recognized her value.

Off to Washington City

What an awakening!

It was not at all what she had expected. The closer the train came to Washington City, the more hesitant Mary felt. Smoke caused by the many fires burning along the rail line filled the air and hovered in the treetops and branches. Soldiers squatted beside them, warming their bodies.

So far, the day was proving to be grim—but Mary faced it resolutely and went on. She had already told so many people at home that this was what she wanted to do. She clutched her surgical bag and walked resolutely toward the first hill of public buildings. The train depot was on New Jersey Avenue, two miles from 17th Street and Pennsylvania Avenue Northwest; about the center of the city.

Once Mary left the train terminal, it was difficult to find her way. Walking was about the only way to get around. She stopped people, ask for directions and followed tall rooftops. She found it all totally exasperating.

Previously, she had read and heard many stories about the soldiers mustering in the Capitol, and about the "overflowing" conditions created by the returning wounded. But she was not prepared for her first sight of Washington's critical condition. All over the city, and as far as she could see miles and miles outward along the Potomac River, there were tents.

It was a city of tents. All sizes and shades of brown tents had popped up, lining the streets and banks of the river. The streets were mushy mixtures of mud and debris from recent rains. Supply wagons moved slowly inward and outward, while rambling along between were white hospital wagons carrying the injured from the battlefields. Squads of soldiers drilled while others idled, resting on the sidewalks or in doorways.

Mary Walker now rationalized that if she wanted to get into the medical arena quickly, she could just volunteer at one of the hospitals and start pitching in. It sounded plausible, but not much of a goal. On her own, she made her way around the city, visiting several of the nearest hospitals. Every large government building available had been turned into a hospital. Rows and rows of beds had been set up, with the average public area containing five hundred beds or more. Stuffed into the corners were cots and pallets for the caregivers to use.

Mary, of course, was seeking a vacancy for a doctor, but found none open to a woman physician. It was not only totally exhausting and awakening, but humbling!

For a moment, Mary caught her breath and closed her eyes. This was not what she had expected. She felt sure no one would fault her if she turned around and went back home. But that was not why she had come. She wanted to prove herself as a doctor. This miserable and pathetic environment would let her do that.

But Mary also wanted the family back home to know she was still resolute. She knew they would be worried, so she wrote them. She told them cheerfully about the places she had been. To Alexandria, on a steamboat that left Washington every half hour. Once there she visited Camp Williams, another tented hospital. On another day, to Arlington Heights, just two and a half miles from Washington.

Through her continuing inquiries, she, at last, learned that the U.S. Patent Office would soon be converted from a make-shift shelter into a hospital, as some parts of the building were not yet completed. Nevertheless, she quickly volunteered to go there—thinking she might be able to get on full time. In the meantime, she could keep looking.

So, at age twenty-nine, Mary Walker swallowed her pride, rolled up her sleeves, and after weighing all her options, volunteered to be a nurse at the Patent Office Hospital.

Chapter 6

Wounded Everywhere

The Patent Office Hospital was operating under the supervision of Dr. J.N. Green. The wounded lay everywhere, dispersed among the glass cases holding numerous American inventions and treasures, including swords, guns, and other inventions dedicated to hostility. Mary wrote her family about the displays instead of the gore. She told them there was even a collection of George Washington's possessions on display. She didn't want them to worry.

From her vantage point in the five-story hospital, Mary could see and hear that the war was escalating. The world around her was in chaos, frightening and disorganized beyond belief.

The schedule at the Patent Office Hospital stayed the same. Wagons came rolling up to the doors continuously, bringing the injured from the train yard. It seemed they were coming from every battle location to Washington. Mary had also read that the poet Walt Whitman was wandering from hospital to hospital, comforting the wounded. It was said he had been entrusted by doctors in the field to supervise train and steamboat trips conveying wounded up the Potomac to the hospitals.

Washington had become a city bustling with war efforts

exhibited on every corner. Mini disasters like shortages of food, transportation, and medical supplies were occurring daily.

The Patent Office offered something of a pictorial refuge. Its regal façade of white marble was yet untouched by mud or blood. It also offered such modern conveniences as hot air and gas heating. Mary felt fortunate that she was given a cot in an alcove and a food ration. Much of the time, however, she found herself falling asleep without even eating a meal.

Thank God that Dr. Green and the nurses were beside her when she faced the first wagon loaded with wounded. Their instructions and manner set a standard for her to follow. She couldn't help but tremble. Their encouraging words mingled with the moans and outcries of the wounded so that she stayed stable and steady on her feet. Her job was to assess the injuries and designate where the patient should be sent for care within the hospital.

Soon she was able to look compassionately into their faces and then at their wounds and send them along with an encouraging word. There was no way that Mary's training at Syracuse, nor her limited practice prepared her for this new and overwhelming experience.

Perhaps it was also fortunate that she had been married. Her experience at medical school had not included much exposure to naked male bodies. Now, she was treating them by the hundreds. Here also, she began to face another medical conflict: *Amputation.* She had already heard that in the field, doctors considered amputation to be the most expedient way to address wounded legs and arms. Generally, hygiene was absent. Infection quickly invaded even the slightest wounds. There just wasn't sufficient time to work with severe limb wounds. Removal was the best approach.

It was probably at the Patent Office Hospital that Mary perfected the elementary techniques of amputation, a medical method she did not approve of except in extreme cases. She made it known that she would avoid it whenever possible. That philosophy continued throughout her career.

Wagonload after wagonload drew up to the side of the Patent Office. Day after day, Mary felt compelled to stay on, and agreed to continue helping Dr. Green. Each day he was beginning to look increasingly tired and overworked. Once, he told her that his supervisor had "worked himself to death," falling ill and dying. No one had been assigned to replace Green, although it seemed only reasonable that someone would soon.

"I'll stay and help until a relief doctor comes," Mary promised. She liked Dr. Green and his family, and was afraid that he too would fall into the same trap as his predecessor and overwork himself.

Chapter 7

Learning the Routine

From her very first days, Mary had taken on the many duties of a volunteer assistant physician and surgeon without any official title or recognition. Her assigned duties involved meeting the ambulances on the west side of the building as they drove up to the hospital and then helping to carry the patients to the top floor of the building. This meant climbing up and down the long staircases many times a day, a physical job as well as a skilled one.

Even when the days and nights became blurred, Mary never lost sight of her goal. She had started working under Dr. Green's supervision in October and before she knew it, it was November. Since she still had not been assigned as either a supervisor or assistant, Mary anxiously asked Dr. Green to write a request to Dr. Clement A. Finley, then Surgeon-General of the United States. Her request was that she be given a definite assignment with Dr. Green. She hoped that in the interim, since writing him some months earlier, the Surgeon General would have changed his mind regarding female doctors.

Mary took the letter to the Surgeon General's office personally, and introduced herself. Upon reading Dr. Green's request, the letter was handed back to her.

"I will not appoint a woman," Finley glared at Mary. "I cannot," he declared. He conceded that there was a grave need for medical personnel, particularly doctors, but he still refused. Mary argued back, reminding him of the hundreds of wounded still laying out there on the battlefields and around the city.

"You can see them everywhere." His reply was the same: "I will not appoint a woman in this capacity."

Not to be outdone, Mary took the letter to the office of an Assistant Surgeon General named Wood. Dr. Wood reviewed Mary's credentials and read the request. He, too, shook his head. "I'm sorry," he said. Reluctantly, he declined to go over his superior's head. But he did indicate that if it were his decision, he would have given Mary the assignment.

Mary reported the situation back to Dr. Green. All he could do was shake his head. "Mary, I'm powerless to pursue this issue further." He explained to her that he, too, was afraid that he might lose his job if he persisted in supporting her request.

Although Mary was totally crushed and disappointed, she agreed to continue acting as his assistant. She was accepted and liked by the patients, and each day continued to make the rounds with a hospital steward, writing down the symptoms of each patient they talked with or examined. Each day, a sizeable group of patients left the hospital with new patients taking their place. By then, a few other nurses, both women and men, had joined the hospital crew, all of them putting up their beds in alcoves like Mary had done and eating whatever food was available.

About one hundred patients would pass through the

hospital each day. Along with wounds from the battlefield, chickenpox and typhoid fever began appearing, passing along from one weakened soldier to another. Identifying the symptoms of chickenpox carriers was essential to keep the disease from spreading throughout the hospital. Mary became an expert at recognizing the first signs of both diseases, and insisting they be kept separated from the other wounded.

A surprise came that winter: a hospital inspection by Superintendent Dorothea Dix. That was part of her job.

Up to now, Mary had not met her. Today, from across the room, Mary was introduced to her. Later, Mary described how she had slowly walked the aisle of beds, noting the way sheets and other materials were being used. She seemed impersonal toward the wounded laying there. Mary felt critical of the fact that she made it all seem routine and did not speak with any of the patients.

God Rest You Merry Gentlemen

The Christmas holiday held little meaning for those stationed in Washington City. Sometimes, Mary would hear a small group of soldiers singing a familiar hymn: "*Peace on earth – goodwill to men,*" and she would hum along with them. She wondered whether anyone really felt the meaning of those words.

Another interesting activity was continuing there in Washington, and Mary was continually watching its progress. Despite the war, carpenters were continuing to work on putting up the dome of the Capitol building. It was an interesting story around Washington, and was often repeated by people as well as the newspapers because it was one of President Lincoln's pet projects.

It seemed that America's first President, George Washington, had approved construction of a Capitol building in July 1793. By 1810, the wings of the building had been completed, but were partially destroyed several months later in the War of 1810. A new architect and a new plan were proposed, and work began again. In 1824, the dome was completed, but no one liked it because it was made of copper.

During the 1850s, Congress began to outgrow the building anyway, and remodeling was begun, using an architectural design that featured a cast-iron dome. By 1861 when this new war began, President Abraham Lincoln insisted that the construction continue, using the iron for fear that it would rust if it laid on the ground until the war was over.

In fact, President Lincoln used this as a metaphor; that the "union would be preserved just as the dome was continuing."

Chapter 8

To Stay or Go?

It was with a heavy heart that Mary, at last, told Dr. Green that she was leaving. Her position there had begun on an informal basis. There continued to be little chance of recognition by the Surgeon General or an appointment by any other commanding general. However, it had not been a totally disappointing experience.

"There is little reason to stay," Mary said. "No one is going to give me an appointment here." She was exhausted from her efforts. At one point, Dr. Green had offered to pay Mary from his own salary, but she knew that would be a hardship to the Doctor, his wife, and his children. "Let me at least see what I can do to help you," he offered.

As the year 1862 neared, Dr. Green contacted everyone he knew. By January, he had found Mary a temporary position as a doctor with the Forest Hill Prison in the Georgetown area of Washington.

And so, Mary undertook a short-term, official medical assignment working with the prison. There were about six hundred men kept there. It wasn't a very complicated job, but it helped Mary earn back a few dollars that she had spent while living at the Patent Office Hospital.

Regrouping

By October, Mary was back home in Oswego, where she picked up her personal crusade where she had left off, and began lecturing around the state again. The crowds were never very large and she didn't make a lot of money, but the fact that she had taken part in the war intrigued many people. Her descriptions and comments drew their attention, particularly from women. Now she could add her observations of the war's ravages on the sick and wounded, and particularly the importance of hygiene in relation to wounds and illness. She rounded out her talks by adding her viewpoint on woman's rights and dress reform.

Speculation had also begun about what would happen to slavery and women's rights after the war ended. Many were convinced that the war would be short-lived.

It was not surprising, then, that many women were now beginning to feel the oppression of being forced to comply to their husbands' viewpoint and will. More women were getting out, many serving in nursing and caregiving positions. More were out attending club meetings and lectures. Some men were already recognizing these disgruntlements; their concession was to let their women folk go to these meetings as long as they were about health issues. The men even dismissed feminist meetings as long as their wives remained quiet with their opinions.

What could be harmful about meetings where women discussed hygiene? They were open to the public and socially approved. Some husbands even felt their wives paid more attention to them afterward.

Each lecture brought in a few pennies, and Mary saved them. She was always wondering how she might broaden her talks.

More education

Yet, Mary was not satisfied with telling, or reading from her handwritten scripts, her same generic stories over and over. Ever restless, she decided to travel to New York City and enroll at the Hygienia Therapeutic College. She had heard many good things about it.

The college was noted for its unconventional type of hydropathic applications, often called water-cure treatment, along with their convalescent therapies. They followed the teachings of J.D. Thall. He and a small group of other doctors there believed that the convalescent period was the most important part of a patient's recovery to good health.

About fifty percent of the college's prior graduates were women. Attendance there also included the opportunity to give lectures at clinics held at Bellevue Hospital. A few weeks later, on March 31, 1862, Dr. Mary Walker received a medical diploma qualifying her to administer their treatment processes.

Through the spring and summer, Mary stayed on at the college. She had become something of a soulmate, bonding with the school's founder Mary Gove Nichols. Their philosophies were much the same. Both women believed that women were better suited than men as caregivers and nurses. There were several other ladies there who shared not only the same health philosophies, but in the pleasure of wearing pants.

One of those women was Susannah Way Dodd, or to her friends, Susan, who was working on her medical degree. Her viewpoint matched Mary's on many topics. All of them encouraged Mary to stay on at the clinic, but she was not content doing what she considered to be rather mundane tasks. It certainly did not compare to her previous active medical practices at the Patent Office Hospital. What she learned at the college fit very strongly with her convictions, but could hardly be applied to battlefield injuries.

"This war, will it never end?" she asked her friends.

The fighting was going on much longer than anyone had ever imagined. Telegraphed reports came in daily and were written up in the newspapers. Everything Mary read about what was happening on the battlefield continued to excite her. She admitted to herself that she was good at being a doctor. Her friends agreed with her. She had been away from the war for eight months. However, fighting had continued on what was called the "western front." Lee's Army was proving much stronger than previously thought.

In New York City and other Eastern cities farther away from the war, the mood seemed to be lighter even though interest was strong. During the year, two serious songs had been introduced and quickly caught on. Julie Ward Howe wrote the *"Battle Hymn of the Republic,"* and George Frederic Root penned the *"Battle Cry of Freedom."* Both became standards and were sung in political and public gatherings, as well as religious and military arenas.

"You're never going to have such an opportunity again unless you go to Europe," friends persistently told Mary.

What they meant, was that there always seemed to be some argument between the European countries that developed into war-like situations. When their quarrels broke out, skirmishes resulted in battlefield wounded. And then the need for doctors soared.

During all this time, Mary had been reading that there were still thousands of wounded soldiers gathered near Warrenton, Virginia, around the site of the Second Battle of Manassas. They were both sick from diseases or recovering from wounds.

The battle had been fought in August, but there was no place to move the wounded. Many still remained where they had been injured, resting under homemade tents, and in nearby barns or houses. But they did have one thing in common, they were all under the command of General Ambrose Burnside.

Chapter 9

Persuading a General

Mary liked what she had read about General Burnside. Like many of the generals commanding in the field, he was a graduate of the U.S. Military Academy at West Point and, after graduation, had served in the Mexican War until 1853. He had returned home to become an arms manufacturer and had invented a highly popular breech-loading rifle. When the war began, he enlisted as an officer with the Rhode Island Volunteers.

After successfully commanding the First Battle of Bull Run, he was promoted to the rank of brigadier general. He also caught the eye of President Lincoln. In the fall of 1862, Lincoln asked Burnside to become commander of the Army of the Potomac. By then, the President and his advisors felt that the war was dragging on too long.

Mary knew that there were other women working in the medical field here and there. In a little sidebar story in one of the newspapers, Mary read that a woman named Clara Barton had set up a hospital tent at the Battle of Antietam, where Burnside's Army had fought earlier.

Mary took this as a good indication that the General must not be opposed to medical women in the field. She decided she would go and meet him. For the occasion, she chose to dress officially as a medical officer, wearing a dark waistcoat over her pants and tying a green medical staff sash around her waist.

Yes, Mary concluded, this was an ideal opportunity to get back into action, either with a commission or working as a public physician. There was little doubt that Mary's previous experiences would give her a strong insight into evaluating such situations. It was obvious, too, that no one else was going to help them. By going to see Burnside, she was expressing her interest. Mary reasoned that meant she would likely be given that assignment as she proposed.

Burnside had gained a reputation as a dashing commander who looked the part by letting his mustache grow into side whispers, later called "sideburns." He was itching to get an attack underway. But his colleagues were begging him to wait.

Now the major obstacle that faced Burnside's troops was that the Confederate troops were camped on one side of the Rappahannock River in Virginia, and the Union troops had dug in throughout and behind the nearby town of Fredericksburg.

The Union commanders had come up with an ingenious plan for crossing the river, but it would take time to put it into action. They had agreed that one way to cross the river was by using pontoon boats, a method that had never been tried before. To protect any work that would be done on the crossing, an elite company of highly trained riflemen called "sharpshooters" would be patrolling along the river, often crossing over and invading sections of the Rebels' lines. While this plan was being put in place, the battle area was generally quiet.

As all of this Virginia region was under Burnside's authority, Mary decided he would be her best contact. Thousands of men had been wounded during the earlier skirmishes and were still out there unattended. But, in addition, Mary learned, many had been sent to their sick beds by a second wave of typhoid fever.

Typhoid was already being recognized as a major opponent for both sides in the war. Often soldiers from both sides would even be found lying side by side, suffering from the fever. Typhoid was a disease Mary already knew something about from her days at the Patent Hospital.

It wasn't an easy trip, but at last Mary succeeded reaching General Burnside's headquarters, and summarized the situation. She recommended that the wounded and sick soldiers be loaded on a train and sent to Washington where she knew first-hand, they would receive better attention.

Burnside immediately liked this sensible doctor that brought him a practical idea on how he could act, removing the wounded, as well as getting them further out of harm's way. He agreed, and wrote out an order giving Dr. Mary E. Walker the authority to accompany the soldiers. She was to receive full cooperation for their transport by train to Washington. Now, was the time to move quickly.

Fighting against time

By the time Mary arrived in Warrenton, Virginia, the group she was concerned about was billeted some miles away in an old house near the town of Manassas. It was evident that the earlier fighting in the town had been done in a manner uncommon to how battles had been conducted up to then. Soldiers had scurried from hiding spots behind houses, to move forward and hide behind fences, woodpiles, and whatever other barriers could be constructed. After contacting the train, Mary immediately began a search for medicine and supplies. There was nothing available.

An effective way to battle typhoid was by applying cool water compresses to the forehead and sometimes over a patient's entire body. Such materials were not available either. Even wooden water buckets had been carried away. Mary scavenged the area, going from house to house, searching for any types of containers to hold the water. Cool water was the only medication at hand. It was plentiful, but there was no way to carry it.

In desperation she asked herself, "What can I do?" even as she knew the answer.

Mary threw open her trunk and ripped up her own cotton night gowns to make the compresses. She instructed medical helpers there to begin moving patients to the rail site and to give every patient a wet compress. While she passed through the town, she purchased several batches of cornbread and brought the food back with her to share.

At last, she was ready to load all of her patients onto the train and send them on their way to Washington. Once there, she knew they would be cared for.

As had been planned, on December 13, Burnside and his generals and a force of 122,000 soldiers advanced to attack General Robert E. Lee's forces across the Rappahannock River.

Doing homework

Before beginning this assignment, Mary had made it a point to learn about the First Battle of Manassas, fought on these same fields a year earlier in July 1861. That first battle had been fought by a Union Army of enthusiast, but naïve young recruits, who were defeated. As the armies of the Union and the Confederacy prepared to meet again, it promised to be a meeting of experienced, seasoned veterans. The plan for the Second Battle was proposed to be carried out over three days from December 11 to 13. But Mary had already learned that dates quickly changed.

In the end, the Battle did not work out as planned. Instead, the campaign opened a gateway for the South's first invasion into the North, sending the Confederate Army to the height of its power.

For Mary, the wait was agonizing. But at last, she received her orders to transport the soldiers away the very day before the Second battle was planned to begin. General Burnside sent a detail of his soldiers to accompany her. The rest of his army would soon follow.

But by then, Mary was on her way to Washington in command of six carloads of casualties and one passenger car of businessmen and politicians —or so she thought. As the sound of train wheels rolling beneath them began Mary breathed a heavy sigh of relief.

But not for long. Only a few miles outside Manassas the train came to a sudden stop. Upon someone's prior orders, an engineer broke off about half of the train and directed it toward Alexandria, Virginia, where skirmishes were occurring. There they sat!

After a delay of some time, Mary inquired what was happening. No one seemed to know. There were no officers left on board. The businessmen in the passenger car were even more puzzled and confused. One passenger was Henry Wilson, a member of the House of Representatives, who in later years was elected Vice President of the United States. He and the others agreed that there might be an imminent danger just setting there. All of them had heard rumors that a small group of raiders had been attacking trains recently. They further agreed that they were certainly an easy target. Mary took that to mean that she had their support.

"Let's go," Mary told the engineer.

She knew that she was interpreting General Burnsides orders to their fullest extent, but glad she had it to rely upon. With that, the train began to move. Again, they were on their way. No one could have been more thankful than Mary.

When the train arrived in Washington,the patients were given sandwiches and turned over to a hospital representative. Mary's assignment was completed. She felt satisfied. This small victory made her feel a great deal more confident in her ability.

Later, many of the soldiers who had been brought to the Patent Office Hospital told the physicians and nurses about being treated by a woman doctor who tore up her night gowns and made compresses, and then bought them cornbread.

"That sounds like Mary, all right!"

Those soldiers that were treated by Dr. Mary and her home spun remedies may have been the lucky ones.

Chapter 10

Battles Begin

Mary had barely arrived in Washington when she was requested to return, this time to Fredericksburg. She was to report to Dr. Preston King, Senior Surgeon for the region. She knew General Burnside was rapidly preparing his forces for another battle in that same area. But neither did she want to walk right into the face of a full-blown conflict. So, she decided to wait a day or two longer and see what would happen next. She could keep abreast of what was happening by telegraphed reports that were being posted.

Although Mary was in Washington only a few hours, she saw that little had changed. In fact, conditions were growing worse.

About that time, news writer Angel Price interviewed the popular poet, Walt Whitman, who was helping out in the war effort. Whitman described his observations as he cared for the wounded soldiers housed around the city. The article was circulated across the country. It repeated exactly what Mary was observing.

"Washington D.C. has become a vast hospital complex caring for more than 20,000 troops. It was all informally run with no privacy or security. A constant stream of people looking for wounded relatives or friends. They moved through the buildings and tents… mothers, wives, sisters of wounded came and cared for them. They were usually accepted by the hospital's nurses. Most hospitals had about 500 beds… many of the buildings were not heated or ventilated…bandages littered the floor… no sanitization of instruments… surgeons sharpened their knives on the side of their boot… blood poisoning, tetanus, and gangrene were common, scurvy and malnutrition were rampant."

The article concluded: "These hospitals were killing as many as they were saving."

There was nothing Mary could do there. She was confident that she would be more helpful in the field. Thousands of wounded and diseased soldiers continued to stream into the field hospitals and encampments from all directions. It was dreary, gloomy, and she saw how depressed all the patients were. She forced herself to give a cheery greeting and to wear a smile everywhere she went.

Keep moving on

In the meantime, throughout the first two weeks of December, Burnside had maneuvered his Army across the Rappahannock River and back again, in preparation for the upcoming battle. These skirmishes also resulted in a staggering number of fresh casualties.

Mary arrived back in Fredericksburg shortly after the battle there had finally been fought, carrying on until December 15, 1862. It was sickening everywhere she looked; it was worse than the previous battle's causalities. The total number of Union soldiers under Burnside and his commanding generals was calculated at 172,504 or more. Another 72,497

Confederate soldiers were on the opposing side, led by General Robert E. Lee.

Chapter 11

Across the River

For practical purposes, it seemed that the battle really began playing out earlier, on December 11. Union engineers had been successful in building the pontoon bridges across the river. The sharpshooters that had been sent ahead to clear the way had also been successful in stopping the advancing Rebel forces.

It was bitter cold and freezing weather, with the effects of snow and ice lingering in the air and on the ground. It was an exhausting undertaking for all the soldiers on both sides. There had been no preparation on either side of the river for removing the wounded out of the area other than having their fellow comrades carry or drag them out. Many simply froze where they fell.

This time Mary was directed to the Lucy House, a sprawling hotel that had been turned into a makeshift military hospital. It was in the same general area as her previous destination, but in the little community of Falmouth. It was cold, and hazy with a winter fog hanging overhead.

Mary was chilled to the bone. But she was warmed by the welcome she received from the Senior Surgeon in charge. He handed her an apron and said, "they're calling it the ghastliest battle of the war." She could barely hear his voice above the screams and cries coming from the wounded that surrounded them.

Mary flinched as her eyes fell on a pile of limbs that had been amputated and thrown out the door to freeze. This was the worst part of war, and a situation she could not even bring herself to acknowledge. In fact, it was almost against her principals. Soldiers from both the Union and the Confederacy lay here, the uniforms of both regulation and militia, gray and blue, mixed together where the battle lines had been overrun.

For her field work, Mary wore the customary field surgeon's cover-up apron that was quickly drenched with blood. Her five-foot frame was all but covered by it. If she was lucky, she would find a plank to stand on so she could give herself height. Here she worked throughout the remainder of December, from bitter cold sunrises until darkness, helping an overwhelming number of wounded.

Over and over, she came face to face with the results of cannons loaded with a combination of metal pieces mixed with small rocks. These rounds of shot literally tore flesh apart, rather than making a clean wound, and the wounds were likely to become infected quickly.

Many doctors, rather than treat such time-consuming wounds, quickly amputated the injured limb. It was said that one casualty per second was wounded in this way in the open cornfields. It was easy to locate and fire upon many soldiers as they crossed them, their identification flag marking their movements. The small metal ammunition shattered bone.

A dreaded skill

And so, Mary Walker began practicing that dreaded skill again, now having learned it very well amputation. She had become a proficient surgeon. Her internship had begun at the Patent Office, and with each stroke of her scalpel she had gained confidence and experience. It was told by reporters who visited the hospital tents that she was compassionate but could perform an amputation in ten minutes. However, Mary never confirmed their stories. She tried to forget them.

It was tiring, it was exhausting, but it brought a sense of satisfaction, even exhilaration, that she had never experienced before. She had always considered herself a humanitarian-- now, in these suffocating surroundings, she was able to give back life and rejoice in her dedication. She appreciated being a surgeon, and felt she could hold her own with the skills of any other surgeon in the field. In these surroundings, she was finding her self-worth.

The battlefield

The battlefields of Virginia spread out over wide open fields, corn rows of tall stately stalks and thick wooded areas. In the sky above rolled thick clouds of smoke that burned the eyes and choked noses and throats. It was difficult to tell exactly where you were located. Some soldiers and local folks called the areas surrounding them by the names of the river and hill tops. Others called them by the names of nearby towns or the names printed on maps.

As an independent agent, Mary traveled back and forth through these acreages, never knowing exactly where she was, but stopping to care for groups of wounded soldiers or a huddle of refugees. Deserted houses, woodsheds, and barns became shelters for the wounded.

It was here, that another enemy became visible: disease. Those felled by disease were probably overlooked and not counted in the war numbers. It was an entirely different environment where the enemy was invisible and the air filled with bacteria, typhoid, flu, and smallpox.

These diseases are the separated partners of every war. They are hidden in the hospital tents and church operating rooms. The stealth of these germs became a challenge for Dr. Mary Walker. She had always been interested in practicing hygiene and good health; this was one of her passions. But a battlefield was not a receptive location.

Outdoor field hospitals were usually set up somewhere in the vicinity of an open field or spotted along the farm hedgerows. Their location was marked out on maps where advance observers had thought the battle might be fought. Mary learned that weeks before a battle, while the generals were still talking, planning, and speculating about what might happen, agents of the Union Army had been sent through the adjoining countryside contracting for farm locations, houses, and buildings that could be converted into hospitals.

These sites were laid out close to water wells or fresh creeks, roads, and traveled lanes. It was arranged with those families, shopkeepers, and ministers that they would move out when the battle started. The injured would then be carried to these shelters for treatment. The fact that the Union lines might be overrun had not been considered, so Confederate soldiers also showed up among the wounded. This made little difference to Mary.

Weather weary

When the weather permitted, hospital tents were usually open on all sides so the light could circulate. Some had flaps that were let down when it rained, snowed, or when the wind was high. Facilities were crude and varied often due to the weather. For example, in the winter, tents that were set up on the bare ground might be heated by digging a trough, covering it over with old railroad iron and earth, then building a fire at one end, and drawing heat to the opposite end.

The wounded were transported to the hospital by whatever means were available. Wooden hospital wagons were built so they could be strung together in trains. Other transports pulled into service included open flatbed wagons, buggies, and buckboards. Many of the wounded walked on make-shift crutches or were simply carried in blankets or on rugs and dumped outside the hospital tent.

If a building was nearby, the doors were removed and turned into stretchers. Even drummer boys had been trained to turn doors into litters to carry one or more wounded.

An estimated 30,000 wounded streamed into the hospital tents set up along both sides of the Rappahannock River. On December 13 alone, 18,000 Northern and Southern soldiers were reported to have been either wounded or killed.

Chapter 12

Chaotic Atmosphere

Following the Battle, and withdrawal of the Union soldiers back across the Rappahannock, soldiers from each side sat along the riverbank exchanging greetings or shouting taunts at one another. After the Battle, it was reported that a northern band started playing and singing Union songs on the east side of the river. After a while, the Confederate soldiers shouted across, requesting that Southern songs be played.

To Mary Walker, it became a strange place to find camaraderie. But it was not unusual.

The veterans on both sides joined in trying to sing away their fears and sadness, but all too soon they were exhausted and weary. Gospel hymns were among the favorites. The battle lines were so close together that they could almost talk to each other.

If Mary had not been busy, she would have witnessed a scene even more emotionally overwhelming than she had seen when she first arrived to work at the Patent Office in Washington. It was a chaotic nightmare surrounding the hospital tents. Years later, historians ranked Fredericksburg as one of the worst battles of the entire war.

In his official report, General Robert E. Lee wrote:

"when night closed in (on Saturday, December 13, at Marge's Heights) the shattered masses of the enemy had disappeared in the town, leaving the field covered with dead and wounded. At one point, the Confederate Army's Brigadier General Williams Barksdale and his forces from Mississippi held the river bank for sixteen hours.

Union Army Major General Ambrose Burnside was forced to withdraw. Having observed the horror of a battlefield covered with the dead and wounded, General Lee was described as sickened by the carnage, and refused to carry the attack further, even though they were in a favorable position to meet and wipe out many more Union soldiers.

In the weeks to follow, General Burnside was replaced by Joseph Hooker, and moved on to command the Army of Ohio.

Mary hardly noticed as she followed the routine set by the other doctors in charge. Her superior, Dr. Preston King, recognized her skills, appreciated her presence, and acknowledged it.

By this time, the "amputation of injured limbs" had become a "hot topic" in medical circles. Surgeons argued long and hard as to the merits of amputation. Two major points that favored amputation were the lack of sanitary conditions and the availability of antiseptic on the battlefield.

The length of time required for transportation to a hospital could range across several days. The lack of care during the trip made it an even greater concern. Even when the patient reached the hospital, amputation was often the prognosis because infection had already set in.

The Medical Service had directed strict rules concerning treatment, and in fact, did encourage amputations as a primary care treatment. Mary had gained experience at the Patent

Office Hospital (which they were now calling the Indiana Hospital), but recognized its value more in the field where the patient had gone for days gathering bacteria, typhoid, or small pox. Amputation was a practice that, for Mary, would have been the opposite from her own preferred holistic practice.

In her conversations with soldiers in the field, Mary did suggest alternative methods to amputation, if they were available. Applying hot poultices helped to draw out infection. She was opposed to amputation, but her dexterity at performing it was under constant observation.

Mary never voiced her opinion, although she had been reviewed several times by both newspaper reporters and other doctors as being adept and skilled at the operation. But the Fredericksburg battle in particular was an example of where a decision to amputate or not was made in seconds. It was vital to ensure that a flesh wound would not become infected and lead to death.

Bacteria was already considered the major killer. A wounded soldier was a prime candidate for infection Additionally, bacteria could not be contained in the churches, schools, houses, and other buildings converted to hospitals, nor to the outdoor tents. The only possible blessing: even hospital tents were beginning to receive quantities of the new pain-killing anesthesia.

Home Again, Home Again
Since Mary was still working at her own expense, she decided to return to Washington in early 1863. Another dismal and lonely holiday season had been spent with injured soldiers, but Mary never made it evident that the situation was intolerable.

Upon her departure, Dr. Preston King wrote a letter to

the U.S. Surgeon General describing the professional duties Mary had performed. He hoped that by doing this some of her expenses would be reimbursed. Despite Dr. King's letter, Mary was not reimbursed, nor was she given a commission.

Yes, it made her angry. None of her battlefield activities were as she had expected. But her resolve and resilience were as strong as ever.

However, it seemed that her experience at Fredericksburg had only proven to strengthen her resolve. All the emotions she had bundled up inside seemed to rise to the surface of her mind. She sometimes caught herself turning cold and beginning to tremble as she thought back. By the time she was ready to return to Washington, she knew she could not face another severe experience like that—at least for a while.

It was a turning point for Mary. She recognized that no matter how much she mended bodies, she still felt helpless, sickened, and tired. She no longer felt self-satisfaction. The excitement gone.

As a contractor or free agent, she decided she needed to escape this misery. Returning to the farm seemed like the only restful solution. Perhaps there she could recover. She could also go back to lecturing around the State. There was a great deal of interest in what was happening on the battlefield. Each lecture brought in a few pennies, and she saved them.

Chapter 13

A Time to Recover

Mary realized that she had to keep working, but she also knew the strength of her physical reserve. Almost by accident, she soon discovered that there were other serious problems being caused by this war. But that would mean returning to Washington.

While she had been working at the Patent Hospital, Mary always seemed to keep running into mothers, daughters, and wives who were either visiting wounded relatives or searching for a son, husband, or brother. All of them, including herself, at some point, had trouble finding a clean and inexpensive place to stay overnight or for a few days. Hotels didn't want them for fear they would be mistaken for prostitutes. Most were usually dirt poor and had no money to tip for services or eat in a hotel's dining room. They were there just to see if they could find or visit a wounded loved one. Upon occasion, Mary had helped one or more find a safe and comfortable place to stay.

An idea begins

Not only were visitors found to be in need, but the war was producing many orphans and unmarried mothers who also sought shelter. Mary was the first to acknowledge that some type of an association could immediately begin helping solve many of these problems.

She sincerely wondered whether anyone else had noticed these poor women wandering around the city. A good way to find out was to ask some of her associates and acquaintances at one of the town hall meetings she was regularly attending again.

Two lecture halls were quite popular in downtown Washington. The Odd Fellow's Hall on Seventh Street and the Union League Hall on Ninth Street had become Mary's regular stops. Sometimes she was even on the program speaking about her observations. On one typical evening, after the regular program, she asked if anyone would be interested in joining with her in finding shelter for these searching ladies. On the spur of the moment, she outlined a plan to rent rooms and make them available to those visiting relatives.

Someone else chimed in: "Did you all hear about the woman who slept under a pine tree next door to the White House because no hotel would accept her?"

As the evening ended, a few pledges were given. This was enough to set Mary impulsively getting the project underway. She felt comfortable extending her skills in meeting people and working with them in a networking fashion.

Organizing such an effort became a monumental challenge. For forty dollars a month she rented a small two-story, gray house near the corner of Tenth Street, across from Ford's Theater. She knew now how to approach people and solicit their help.

Among her next stops was a visit to the General Command's Headquarters. There she enthusiastically laid out her plan and proposal to General Edward R.S. Canby, who was in command. By now she was accustomed to talking to generals.

Mary's remarks were a familiar story to the General. His office was badgered daily for information about the whereabouts of wounded soldiers. At the prospect of solving that problem, the General welcomed her idea and even gave her permission to scavenge his headquarters for cooking utensils, worn and torn blankets and sheets, broken furnishings, and anything else usable. He even gave her soldiers and wagons to carry her gatherings.

Growing success

Next, she moved on to contact Major General Daniel H. Rucker. His rank made him second-in-command of the city's Quartermaster's Bureau of the War Department. He was a veteran of thirty years and recognized the fear many people had for the rabble of soldiers sprawling around the city. From him she sought the security she needed to transport these women through the streets. He, too, agreed to help her.

Mary patted herself on the back for having succeeded in obtaining their support and cooperation in implementing her plan.

It was quickly developing, but she needed even more volunteers. Surprisingly, she discovered that Washington did not have any comparable church or public service organizations. She wrote and handed out announcements and took out a newspaper ad announcing that she was starting an association to work on this problem in an organized and formal manner.

A few more women came to the next meeting and an election was immediately held to select officers. Based on her experience with the Dress Reform group in Rome, Mary knew how much time and energy it would take to make the newly established "Women's Relief Association" work. Yes, hours and hours.

With her usual characteristic enthusiasm and energy, Mary threw herself into getting the Relief Association and the Home off the ground. Experience had taught her to first get the Home established and then let the Association's vice president take over keeping it operating. Mary particularly appealed to church women and doctor's wives. Many of these volunteers were also in a position to sponsor the kind of fund-raising events that appealed to prominent Washingtonians. Money was always a necessity!

Once many of the ladies were involved, they became generous sponsors. It was obviously an undertaking that frequently drew praise or compliments from their peers and the newspapers. Mary welcomed them, and urged them to take over the organizational responsibilities to which they could apply any of their own ideas.

At long last, she was pleased by all her efforts.

Two other groups that grew out of these troublesome times were The Women's Christian Association and the Women's Hospital and Soldier's Orphan Home. Their combined efforts helped to meet the growing needs within the city.

Moving on

It was now time for Mary to move on. Her feeling of self-satisfaction probably caused her to sing a few lines of a song she knew and sometimes recited in a lecture:

"No foot of land do I possess, No cottage in this wilderness where I can sing Home sweet home."

Again, it was time for Mary to take another break of a few weeks and return to her parents' home in Oswego. There she could sit and marvel at the success of her past several weeks' activities.

She left behind one little problem. As a part of her plan, Mary had also taken a few of the visitors into her own home on Tenth Street. Much like her parents did, she opened it to friends and many visitors she did not know. Even when she was away at the war front or lecturing, her home was used by others who needed shelter. This occasionally caused anxieties, as often these comforts went unappreciated. That was always a worrisome thought.

By now, it was late June, 1863. It was still an intense time of uncertainty, but the war continued. Mary believed she was one of the few women doctors practicing in Washington—maybe the only one. She felt a sense of obligation. However, by now, there were several women who had earned their medical degrees.

Chapter 14

Making Friends

By now Mary had come to know President Abraham Lincoln very well. She, along with Susan B. Anthony and many of the other suffragists had campaigned vigorously for his election to a second term. The White House was open to the people and had become a gathering location for politicians, military personnel, lobbyists. and even the general public.

"Just walk right in. It's the people's House," was the unspoken invitation."

Mary was always excited to be invited to these gatherings and other parties that were held around Washington. She had met Mary Todd Lincoln many times and liked her very much. From the beginning, Mary had considered herself to be a Democrat, but sometimes she couldn't help but speak more from an Independent's perspective.

For these occasions, Mary wore her long dark frock coat over her pants and curled her hair so no one could mistake her for a man. Often, she wore a vest and black bow tie. Through the winter she had worn an overcoat reinforced with a lining. She sometimes wore a small black hat with feathers in front, or in the summer a brimmed straw hat with a ribbon. She still liked her blue Army uniform with striped pants and green doctor's sash.

Many suffragists were now choosing to wear white dresses. To many women in the suffragists' ranks, white meant purity. To others it represented unity or solidarity. Mary was reluctant to wear white, as she wanted to be as independent as she chose. She wanted to stand out and be recognized for her value.

By now, Mary was well acquainted with a wide number of people from varying backgrounds including the military, elected government officials, politicians, and lobbyists. She was pleased that many of them recognized her as well. She was positive that they probably whispered to their companion, "there's that radical woman doctor who wears pants."

Here she stood, a plain woman with an occasionally caustic tongue. She enjoyed the banter back and forth with them. No one was more vocal about her wearing pants than General William Tecumseh Sherman, whom she had met on numerous occasions. She considered him to be one of her strongest supporters.

"Why don't you wear proper women's clothing, Mary?" He always greeted her with a pleasant challenge about her attire.

"Your toggery is neither one thing nor the other."

On one occasion he had teased by flat out asking her, "When are you going to give up wearing those pants?"

Mary usually favored the General with a spirited smile and toss of her curls. They had each felt the winds of war. She loved him for his remarks, enjoyed his teasing, and equally enjoyed talking with him about aspects of the war or politics. She didn't consider it flirting.

During these visits, she again found that the listening skills she learned from her father proved invaluable. Conversing with military men had become one of her better skills.

It was also common to see the President out and around Washington City, riding or taking a drive in his carriage. On more than one day, Mary had seen him and his son riding in the early mornings.

It was not surprising then, that on May 4 Mary had seen him outdoors at a gathering at the Sixth Street Wharf greeting one of his favorite generals. On that day, she paid particular attention to his face. It was beginning to show the stress of these many years of War. He was beginning to show what the newspapers were calling "careworn cheeks."

The excitement of war

Although Mary had taken a year off, the war had not. It still crept on. She had soothed her desire to work in social issues, and she was proud of her success. But she had not found the exhilaration and excitement that being on the battlefield had given her.

She was reluctantly sure she would go back—but when and where? She had continued her efforts by letters and inquiries to obtain a commission, but nothing seemed promising. She had not abandoned her goal, but maybe she could give it a new twist.

Spontaneously, she announced: "I'll start my own Army! We will be called U.S. Patriots!"

Mary was ecstatic about her idea. She didn't believe this was a wild or preposterous proposal.

She declared that she would organize her Army along the same lines that many of the Confederate landowners had done. Many of those officers had begun by giving themselves a rank of Colonel and recruited their tenants into their regiment. In Medieval times, knights had formed their armies in the same way, by recruiting poor young men who wanted to learn to fight.

Mary pointed to her success in forming the Women's Benefit Association. When she worked at the Patent Office Hospital, soldiers had even referred to her as "the soldier's friend."

On November 2, 1863, Mary proposed her plan in a letter to Secretary of War Edwin Stanton. She laid out her plan. She envisioned forming a regiment of soldiers whose enlistments were over, and who, she felt, she could convince to re-enlist in her Army. After all, many of the soldiers who were already serving in the War had built their regiments around an active physician.

Secretary Stanton wasted little time in rejecting Mary's offer. Mary again felt a moment of exasperation. So must have Secretary Stanton. He knew that woman, and Mary Walker could certainly be annoying!

Along the way

Mary always seemed to have a survival plan lurking somewhere in the back of her mind. Not to be outdone, and dis- playing her usual bold spirit, she next wrote directly to President Abraham Lincoln. In a letter dated January 11, 1864, she pointed out that she had been denied a commission solely because of her sex and that had she been a man, a star would have been taken from the heavens and awarded to her.

This time she did some homework and specifically asked for an assignment at the Douglas Hospital in the female ward—but she would prefer an extra surgeon's commission and permission to go anywhere she might be needed. A commission would give her the rank of lieutenant and an increased salary to one hundred five dollars a month.

President Lincoln replied personally, writing his rejection as a note on to the bottom of Mary's letter. Once again, bitter tears filled her eyes. She refused to cry. She refused to be defeated. Now even her friend, the President, had denied the commission she knew she was qualified to receive. She recognized her own value and was furious.

Friendship returns

Almost like a miracle, a response came from another unexpected source. During these many months, Mary had also continued writing to friends and acquaintances, asking them to make contacts on her behalf. She had written again to Secretary of War Stanton and to other past associates, one of which was Dr. Robert C. Wood from the Patent Office Hospital.

Wood indeed sent a letter of commendation to John Franklin Farnsworth, his Illinois senator. He pointed out that for two years under his supervision, "Mary had been active, efficient and very useful in her ministering to the sick and wounded soldiers in this department."

He went on to urge the Congressman to find a good position where Mary could properly support herself. Mary appreciated these pleas on her behalf, and at the same time, she also wrote another letter to Secretary of War Stanton to let him know that she was once again available.

Whatever had been the point of influence Mary did not know, but she was soon authorized to report to the Assistant Surgeon General in Chattanooga, Tennessee for an evaluation.

Mary wondered what he meant. Evaluation? She felt a flash of rebellion, and decided to take her time in going there.

Chapter 15

A Free Spirit

One never knew what Mary might do as she traveled around the countryside on her way to any new assignment. She considered herself something of a "free agent volunteer," particularly when she was paying her own way. She also seemed to travel on her own time clock. Her stops along the way to look over hospitals or health care homes were unpredictable.

It didn't really seem to bother Mary that the war might be passing her by. She considered herself in the war, but in her own way. She had read closely about U.S. Grant's battle in Vicksburg, Mississippi, in May, but that wasn't within the scope of her assignment.

She may have convinced herself that because she had received permission to do certain activities, that meant she could do whatever she chose to do. It did appear that when she gave an order, it was carried out.

On one particular day, she decided she would go visit a deserters' prison in Alexandria, Virginia. She had heard a rumor that the facility was unhygienic. She dressed in the medical officer's uniform she had made for herself. A gold stripe ran the length of the pants from waist to ankle, and a green sash flowed from her shoulder. Her hair was in curls and she wore a felt cavalry hat instead of a cap.

"I'm Dr. Walker of the Union Army," she announced. "Let me pass." Her demeanor certainly convinced the doorkeepers.

Once inside she treated a few soldiers and discovered that several other soldiers were being unjustly held. She promptly sent word about the situation to Secretary of War Edwin Stanton. She then departed with the same jaunty spirit.

Who was this woman who came and went as she pleased? Everyone was left to wonder.

Onward toward Tennessee

As the fall approached, Mary continued on to her assignment in a region near the Chattanooga, Tennessee battlefront. The weather was nice and she was taking her time.

As she approached the area, she began to hear stories of what had taken place at a battle they were now calling the Battle of Chickamauga, that had been fought in September. It had been one of the bloodiest battles thus far, with tens of thousands of soldiers still laying wounded in the surrounding countryside.

Mary could not have arrived at a better time. The assistant surgeon of the Fifty-Second Ohio Volunteers of the Army of the Cumberland had died in January and no one had replaced him. Hearing this, Mary could barely believe her good fortune. In her mind, there certainly wasn't time for an evaluation as had been instructed.

As was her custom, Mary reported directly to the area commanding officer, Major General George H. Thomas, now known to his soldiers as the "Rock of Chickamauga." He instantly liked this determined young woman, and after talking with her about her experiences, forthwith appointed her a civilian contact surgeon for the Fifty-Second Ohio.

General Thomas' was well known for his concern for his soldiers, as well as the wounded. This was demonstrated by the fact that he set standards for his hospital service, where chloroform was readily used in surgery, and railroad cars had been converted to rolling field hospitals.

The practice for using the chloroform antiseptic was to cover a funnel with cloth, and the medication dripped onto a cone of cloth, helping the patient to fall asleep. It was then removed, and a hand fan was used to fan any vapors away from the surgeon or staff. Once a surgery was completed, fresh air was fanned onto the patient's face, driving the vapors away.

Meeting the needs

General Thomas immediately sent Mary on her way with an escort to Gordon's Mill, southeast of Chattanooga. There she reported to Major General Alexander McCook. He welcomed her as a God send. He knew there were hundreds, if not thousands, of wounded soldiers recovering throughout the area. He knew that would keep Mary busy.

"Get busy and apply your skills," he told her. Quickly, Mary responded by tying a surgeon's apron around her waist and began assisting the other medical staff already there.

The first to protest Mary's presence with the Fifty-Second Ohio was a certain Dr. Perin, the medical director of the Army of the Cumberland.

"Never will I approve a woman doctor. Never!"

He raged on in protest and anger. He challenged her capabilities and skills, and ordered that she be questioned by a panel of four other doctors. Mary agreed to meet with them, even though they all knew that her presence had become a political issue. The discussion soon took on the form of an inquisition.

They questioned Mary; she answered them back in a spunky, caustic tone. They rated her skills not much higher than a housewife's and questioned whether she had really studied medicine. They criticized her for being an eclectic healer who used herbs and home remedies. They criticized her as a woman.

Mary refused to hold her tongue. She fired back her views of how unhygienic they were keeping their hospitals. In the end, she shrugged off their comments. It stung her pride, but she did not show it. She squared her shoulders and went back to her duties. She knew there were doctors who supported and agreed with her, particularly on the topic of performing amputations.

Ignoring the Board's report, Major General McCook ordered Mary to continue her work at Gordon's Mill. There were too few doctors and nurses in the field. It was not a time to quibble. In the presence of other officers, he praised Mary for her willingness to serve in his command. He liked what he saw in this feisty, spirited woman, and he saw the good effect she had on his soldiers. McCook went even further. He praised her to their commander, Major General Thomas, who had hired Mary, so that he, too, became an admirer.

Mary was elated in her new position, although it came at a time when the troops under her care and in the regiment were regaining their strength and many were heading back to their original outfits. This could not be said for the war-weary people out in the small surrounding communities where medical help was not available. In addition to the military, Mary continued administering to such civilian needs as delivering babies, setting broken bones, and helping those still recovering from typhoid in both Union and Confederate families.

Days passed, soon turning into weeks. Mary made a point of continuing to wear her surgeon's uniform on to the field and to treat everyone who crossed her path. She ate with them. She slept with them in a shelter or out under the stars. She treated them for every illness, and often threw in helpful cooking and sewing tips. She wanted to reassure them that she was a capable physician.

One trick that Mary often shared was to resew the shirt collars on uniforms. It seemed that the insides of collars were not sewn smoothly, creating neck burns and sores. This simple courtesy gained her many friends.

Still a free agent

By every measure Mary Edwards Walker was a doctor. Still, she was a free agent. As a civilian contact surgeon, she would be entered on the paymaster's books to receive one hundred dollars a month. Nurses were paid more, some as much as twenty dollars per day. It wasn't that Mary felt she was being greedy, but she felt her rank was the equivalent of a first lieutenant.

At Gordon's Mill, she was assigned a sleeping room in the kitchen of the nearby miller's home. To Mary's way of thinking, that meant there might also be a hearty meal or two thrown in. Understandably, Gordon's Mill became her next "Home Sweet Home." During this time, Mary surely shared her joy in a silent prayer. She loved what she was doing and showed it in how she treated the people.

Chapter 16

In the Field

During the time that Mary was with General McCook's Army of the Cumberland, she tried her best to work at a distance from Dr. Perin and his medical board friends.

"No, sir," she didn't want to tangle with them again.

With General McCook's approval, Mary was now able to wander to and from hospital sites and out into the country side where she continued treating the farm families and townspeople alike. She continued to find wounded soldiers clustered in old barns still recovering from wounds, and patches of chicken pox or typhoid springing up without warning. These all had to be treated.

Mary was given a horse to ride, as well as a wagon, which she seemed to prefer, and an assortment of Union Army medical supplies to use. She treated everyone whether they were Union or not. Sometimes she had an escort, but most of the time she traveled alone, wearing her surgeon's green sash across her jacket to identify her rank.

She occasionally wandered behind the enemy lines, but her friendly approach and her offers to help generally dispelled any concerns.

In the evening, she usually reported back to the miller's

home or the General's headquarters. Often, she retold some of the community gossip she may have heard. Some of her acquaintances around the camp considered her actions to be those of a spy. She resented that label and considered most of what she heard and passed along to be the "talk of a gossip." Everyone recognized her friendly nature. She liked to talk and ask questions, there was nothing secret about that! Sources of a political nature thought otherwise.

One day, she reported she had been stopped by a group of tough looking riders, some wearing gray pants.

"What's your purpose out here?" the leader had demanded.

Mary pointed back at a farmhouse. "I've been treating a family back there," she replied. "They are recovering from typhoid," she said, knowing that with that information they would not go down to investigate.

"I've sworn only to kill blue coats, not doctors," the leader had laughed. "Nor women."

He waved his hat and shushed Mary's horse along. "On your way."

"You must have met up with Champ Ferguson," the soldiers told her. "You're darn lucky. He's a marauder and doesn't belong to anyone's army."

Mary was well liked by the soldiers around the headquarters. They knew she liked to gather herbs and moss for medicinal purposes. Sometimes when they were escorting her, she would share berries she had picked.

"You had better get a revolver and carry it with you," more than one soldier advised. They helped her select one and showed her how to use it.

In fact, Mary selected two revolvers and sometimes wore the brace in a holster over her uniform. But they were cumbersome and a lot heavier than she had thought they would be. Her alternative was to carry them in a pouch and take them out whenever she thought they might be needed.

Sadly, she learned in the next days that maybe she should have been wearing one when the unexpected happened. At least she could have pulled gun out and flourished it.

Surprised and off-guard

Mary enjoyed being outdoors and riding or walking through the woods. The countryside had more trees growing than the farmlands in New York.

On April 10, 1864, dressed in full medical uniform, Mary set off on one of her customary trips, riding alone along a marked trail crisscrossing the woodlands. Unknowingly, she crossed the boundary into Georgia. Overhead the pines towered, and she could smell their scent. Below them, the lower growing oak branches were beginning to show silvery green leaves. It was spring, and some white dogwood and redbud were beginning to bloom. Their tiny blue flowers hugged the grass, interspersed with yellow dandelion blooms.

Mary may have remembered that this was the trail where she previously had found young dandelions, poke, or burdock weeds growing. Although it was still early in the season, she thought she might find moss to make a good poultice. These medicinal items would refresh her medicine chest.

She also looked for mushrooms or ripening wild strawberries that would complement her diet. Right now, their tender green leaves could be chopped into a salad or cooked down like a spinach.

It was turning into a good trail for Mary, and maybe she was concentrating too much on the path and the kinds of plants growing there.

"Halt."

Suddenly a shout rang out at her. Mary stopped, startled as a Confederate sentry popped out from a thick stand of trees. Two more soldiers appeared, all pointing rifles at her. They had also been walking in the same direction along the south side of the Georgia-Tennessee border, south of the town of Chattanooga.

The sentry immediately recognized Mary as the "lady doctor" that they had heard about. From his reactions, Mary knew he considered her a worthy captive and would be taking her in. She would not be able to talk herself out of this unfortunate meeting, but she tried.

"I'm a doctor," Mary explained. "I've been treating families nearby."

He wasn't listening to her story. She could feel his excitement. "I'm taking you to headquarters, Ma'am, Let's go." When they reached the Confederate headquarters, the sentry became a hero, and the news of Mary's capture was telegraphed ahead.

By the time Mary was taken before the commanding officer, General Daniel Harvey Hill, heknew that he had captured a prize. Her reputation proceeded her. She was the doctor who insisted upon wearing a man's uniform.

It just so happened that Mary was captured on a day when General Hill's career was at its peak and he was looking for opportunities to increase his political favor with the President of the Confederacy, Jefferson Davis.

General Hill immediately decided he would send his prized prisoner directly to Richmond, Virginia, where the Confederacy had established its headquarters and a prison system. He knew this would make good conversation among the other officers and that news of her capture by his men would travel around numerous Confederate encampments, adding to his reputation.

Mary had heard of General Hill as well; after all, the circle of officers on either side of the conflict was rather small. It was said that he was the hardest fighting officer in the Southern Army, but that he was arrogant and often outspoken, making him his own worst enemy. A West Point graduate who had already excelled as an officer in the Mexican War (1846 to 1848), he felt his strategies for winning certain battles were being ignored.

Hill had already been made a major general, then promoted to lieutenant general, but he kept squabbling with President Jefferson Davis over his present rank. He had been given the full rank of General only a few days before Mary's arrival.

As the two prepared to go their separate ways, Mary heard the news that General Hill had suddenly lost his new command due to his continuing difficulties with President Davis. He was leaving the Army and returning to his home.

Mary scolded herself again for falling into the hands of the enemy; had she not met such an ambitious individual as General Hill, she might have been able to talk her way out of going to prison on the basis of her being a doctor.

Mary had heard nothing but bad things about the Richmond prison. It had once been a model encampment. Now times were tough, if not terrible, there and she knew she could expect no leniency. But the most promising news was that most officers who were sent there were being exchanged within a few months.

Mary also learned that the most recent commander had been relieved and better conditions were expected. He had been a barbaric officer named George W. Alexander. A Naval officer before the war, he had resigned from the U.S. Navy and enlisted in the Confederate States Army as a private. His rank had soon been returned, along with new responsibilities in Richmond's prison system.

Alexander had lived up to his "black beard" reputation, wearing tight black trousers buckled at the knee. A loose black shirt with a white collar was complimented by a black beard. He was accompanied on his rounds by a mean, black Bavarian boar hound. The lashing of prisoners was common as a major disciplinary measure.

When she heard that news, Mary shuddered, and prepared herself for the long march to Richmond with only the clothes on her back, her medical bag, and whatever blankets and materials she could snatch or beg or barter from the supply wagon. However, this time Mary traveled by train where groups of people gathered along the rail tracks to catch a glimpse of her.

Gossip traveled fast. A woman doctor had been captured!

Chapter 17

Castle Thunder

Originally nicknamed "Castle Thunder," as the prison had been set up to house three types of prisoners and evil doers, but as the years had passed, the mix of prisoners had changed.

Actually, Castle Thunder was a complex of three converted tobacco drying warehouses clustered on Cary Street near downtown Richmond. They were located between Cary and 18th Streets about two blocks from Libby Prison, which also served as the major compound for prisoners.

Together the three tobacco buildings resembled a "parallelogram" with the largest – Gleanor's warehouse in the front. It was three stories tall. Palmer's Factory and Whitlock's Warehouse were attached to either side. A high wall had been constructed to connect the two wings in the rear and provide an open area that could be used as an exercise yard. The collective compound had been named Castle Thunder because many of the people passing outside along the roadway said it resembled the Tower of London. Cells with barred windows had been built inside the buildings to hold condemned men or criminals awaiting trial.

Mary was met by the area commander, Captain Joseph Semmes, who later wrote his wife, telling her that he had met

Dr. Walker. He wrote that he "had been both amused and disgusted at the sight of a debased Yankee woman in pants." At their first meeting, he had smiled cordially and waved her inside along with the other captives.

Accommodations were bleak, worse than Mary had anticipated. She walked slowly through the buildings, critically evaluating and assessing every wall of her new surroundings. Bare walls offered little insulation; wooden troughs served as toilet facilities. It was early spring and daylight was beginning to last longer. Dim gas lamps hung on the walls here and there. The other prisoners said they were used sometimes, but in reality they looked as though they had never burned at all. Nearly all of the water buckets Mary saw were empty.

Horror coming true

All the bad stories that Mary had heard or been told about Castle Thunder seemed to be horribly true.

In early April, Mary's capture and transport along with other prisoners had been telegraphed to the Richmond newspapers. When Mary Walker walked into Castle Thunder, she must have felt like she was walking into Hell. A crowd of curious prison watchers gathered near the entrance to get a glimpse of her and shouted at her as she entered the prison. From the beginning, Mary found herself both a prisoner and a curiosity.

She was also hungry. By the time she arrived there were no rats nor beetles left to eat in the compound. One cup of brown beans, often mixed with bugs or worms, was given to each prisoner daily. Sometimes there was cornbread. Scraps of food could be bought. At night the gas lamps were turned off, and Castle Thunder became a frightening freak house where prisoners attacked one another and abuse went unnoticed or ignored by the guards and administrators. Prisoners were on their own to protect themselves.

Days passed meaninglessly until the warmer, humid summer temperatures set in. The prison was a breeding ground for germs and the circulation of several types of diseases that thrived on the weakened health of the prisoners. Diarrhea was always present, but other diseases included smallpox, typhoid fever, and diphtheria

Mary knew all of these. All of this contributed to the miserable conditions, which under the darkness of night compounded into an unsafe, and frightening surroundings. Murders were reported. There was abuse, rape, and beatings that generally went undetected. There was little escape for either men or women, and few places to hide.

Mary could do little to defend herself except hide by night and keep her distance from certain prisoners. She realized immediately that this was not a social atmosphere. She silently prayed that her prison time was being counted and that she would be recognized and released soon.

Good intentions gone

The original intent of the Confederate administrators was that the Union officers sent to the Richmond prison would be sheltered, treated, and fed as they would have been treated in the field. But after two years of war, good intentions had vanished. A slight improvement occurred shortly before Mary arrived, when Lucien W. Richardson was assigned the prison's new commander. But little else changed.

Prisoners had to endure poor ventilation and foul air. Nights were the worst, filled with abuse. Cries and threats echoed out of the darkness from the time the sun set until the first light of the next day. As early summer came in Virginia, temperatures began ranging into the seventies and upwards inside the closely shaped buildings of Castle Thunder.

Water was at a premium. The buckets were refilled at the leisure of the guards. Much of the time, the water troughs were dry.

From the first day Mary entered the prison she took it upon herself to annoy the gate keepers, shouting at them for medical supplies, better food, and cleaner conditions, generally to no avail. She also began filing complaints about the food and living conditions. She felt that was her obligation as a doctor, even though she knew it would have no effect. On a good day, the prisoners might expect beans and rice. No utensils were available so most items were eaten by the handful.

As a home gardener she pointed out that there were probably already some kinds of vegetables being raised on the farms in the area. But only now and then were a few vegetables handed out. Winter stored cabbage was sometimes added. Mary hoped that her pleas would create a little sympathy toward a woman. They all had mothers, maybe sisters or wives.

For prisoners with an officer's rank or reputation such as Mary, some small necessities could be purchased or traded. Mary's notes home were cheery, optimistic that she would be there only two to four months. She was hopeful that her family would read between the lines. They did, and sent her some money to use for trading with the guards.

It was reported that one time when she became ill, she used some of that money to buy raw eggs from the commissary to eat. She thought they would ease her stomach pain.

Mary was quick to recognize the advantages of being

strange and different at a time when there was little to keep people entertained. She soon learned that she had been singled out by camp leaders or designated as a curiosity, meaning she made good copy and was being frequently written about in the *Richmond Examiner* and other local papers.

These reports drew at least one invitation for her to take tea and little cakes with the wives of the prison's administrators. They wanted to meet this woman doctor who was defying the customary dress code and wearing an officer's clothing.

Perhaps this was her first inkling that publicity could be valuable. So, she was pleasant and witty to those who were curious, and thankful for the sips of tea and bites of cake they served at their event.

Playing the game

Reportedly, Mary coaxed the guards to let her out onto the sidewalk now and then where she would walk or sometimes jumped rope for any curious prison watchers.

Prison chaplain Rev. J. L. Burrows also confirmed to the newspapers that because of her unusual position there, Dr. Mary was sometimes permitted to stroll outside the prison on the street. There she took advantage of her freedom to skip about, pulling up her skirt and displaying her pants, and boots.

Her outings always assured her a following of children with whom she enjoyed chatting. Sometimes she would sing a hymn, so the guards would say. Again, these opportunities were not lost by the newspaper reporters who were always looking for a quick anecdote.

In another issue, the *Examiner* reported that a child had been seen looking out one of the prison windows waving a small Union flag. Later, it was confirmed that it was really Dr.

Mary, who due to her petite size and weight loss had been mistaken for a child. Indeed, Mary was learning to recognize the usefulness of public relations, and demonstrated it whenever she could.

Making good copy

Yes, Dr. Walker made good copy for the *Examiner*. There were a few other women imprisoned there. Many were thieves; others were even dressed in men's clothing or uniforms.

On one occasion, it was reported that Mary "got mad, pitched into several of her room-mates in long dresses, and tore out handfuls of auburn hair from the head of one of them." On another occasion she proclaimed secession, and went into another room where she supposedly installed herself as "lady and lioness of all she surveys."

One day the paper reported that "sometimes she exhibits herself in costume on the balcony of the Castle." It was also gossiped that she had a Yankee major lover among the prisoners at the Libby Prison, which was one square below the Castle, and within easy signal range. She, for one, was not forgotten.

One thing, however, that annoyed Mary was that the reporters persisted in calling her dress pants "bloomers," even though they were a redesigned version of her original pants. Really, they were more of a trouser with a skirt over them. Mary tried to explain this to them, but no one really cared nor wanted to read a newspaper's correction.

Another blessing for Mary may have been the construction of the Reform Dress Underwear that she designed and wore. They were protective and difficult to remove. Even more so off a woman kicking and flailing about.

Originally, the underwear's design had been emphasized because it buttoned at the rear with the intention of preventing rape. Mary was five feet tall and weighed about 120 pounds when she entered Castle Thunder. She gradually began to lose weight until her slight frame resembled a potato sack of eighty pounds

Chapter 18

Counting the Days

Castle Thunder was considered a high-risk prison. But by the time Mary arrived, its occupants had become a mixture of Union soldiers, deserters, political enemies, and civilians. It had been reported that about one hundred women had been placed there after capture as soldiers or spies.

A hospital was a part of the prison makeup, but early upon her arrival the administrators told Mary they had their own doctors and a set of rules for treating patients. Although she never formally became part of the prison's caregivers, she kept her medical bag with her and was able to help persons in need as she found them; kind words and a prayer were likely the only medicines available.

Mary was a pest, she knew it. But it didn't stop her. The *Examiner's* editor even responded with a compliment, calling her a "sensible female."

Mary had always considered herself to be strong, but she could feel her health beginning to deteriorate as a result of the starvation. She had been imprisoned for seventy-three days when she met the Reverend J.T. Carpenter, a Confederate chaplain, who visited with the prisoners, praying with them and offering comfort when he could.

It was on June 22, 1864, that he inscribed his name on the front page of a pocket-sized Bible and gave it to Mary. Thereafter she began reading the Bible daily and carried it with her out of the prison. From it, she gained hope, some comfort, and strength. Upon occasion, she would recite a verse, perhaps:

"I can do everything through Him who gives me strength." Philippians 4:13

When she thought it would be effective, Mary continued writing a few short letters and smuggling them to newspapers, politicians, and military officials, calling attention to her imprisonment and the horrible conditions of the prison. *The Richmond Whig* newspaper confirmed that Mary had previously smuggled out letters to northern newspapers describing the horrendous conditions in Castle Thunder. In July 1864, she wrote a request to meet with Brigadier General William Montgomery Gardner, Commander of all Confederate military prisons east of the Mississippi River and the new provost marshal of Richmond.

He agreed to talk with Mary. Upon their meeting, he could not help but admire the courage of this whisp of a woman who still showed so much pent-up spirit and self-awareness of her military standing. She recited to him the explicit conditions existing inside the walls of Castle Thunder, and its failure to live up to even the most common of health standards.

He had only to look at her haggard face surrounded by dry, coarse hair to know she spoke the truth. She had gathered her courage for this meeting and spoke to him in her man-to-man manner. She emphasized to him her own failing health since arriving there only a few months earlier. She noted that her eyes were deteriorating from mold or damp bacteria; that her obvious weight loss, teeth, and gum conditions were caused by poor food rations. She pointed out that her prison companions were in equal or worse condition.

General Gardner had arranged this meeting because he was annoyed by the press she had attracted—but now, true or false, he recognized her failing health. He suggested that if she wanted to avoid some of the stress caused by the news people, she might wear a more "feminine garb."

At that remark Mary's patience gave way and her temper flared. She squared her shoulders and retorted back that *"women have no more right to be dictated to by men than men have to be dictated to by women."*

General Gardener left both impressed and sorrowful. He signed Mary's release request papers on August 12, 1864. In her weakened condition, Mary was suddenly overwhelmed, tears streamed from her eyes in thanksgiving. When at last alone, she held her Bible tightly and thanked God for this deliverance.

For the remainder of her life, Mary Walker never spoke nor elaborated as to what may have happened to her while she was imprisoned in Castle Thunder.

Released

Mary's 's release was confirmed when she was told that she would be among two dozen or more Union doctors that would be exchanged.

To accomplish this, Mary and a group of officers were transported aboard the steamer *New York* down the James River from Richmond to Fortress Monroe, then taken safely behind the Union lines and exchanged. Ordinarily, she might have been sent down the James River to City Point (later becoming the town of Hopewell) where official exchanges were usually made. But this exchange was considered different. On August 10, 1864, Mary was exchanged "man for man" or "officer for officer."

Recognition of this equality brought her a great deal of personal satisfaction. If there could be any pleasure drawn from her four months' experience at Castle Thunder, that was undoubtedly it.

"Free at last." She could not wait to take a bath and wash every thought of Castle Thunder from her body forever. Clutching her Bible and medical bag, Dr. Mary Walker proudly walked out of Castle Thunder and a horrifying chapter in her life.

Chapter 19

A New Challenge

Mary truly believed that a challenging new chapter was beginning for her. She wanted desperately to put the events of the past four months behind her. She was determined not to spend time reviewing a horrible experience or speaking further about her captivity in Castle Thunder.

For a vocal, rebellious young woman, this was very much out of character. But it was obvious that this was an event in her life that she chose to banish from her mind, strongly wishing to forget it. Even later in her life, at those times when the issue arose, she chose to repeat a formal statement: "I chose not to discuss it."

Regaining her health and getting on with her job was now uppermost in Mary's mind. However, she did keep the Reverend Carpenter's Bible with her and read from it regularly. She felt positively that her faith had been strengthened.

"I will do this every day for the rest of my life," she promised herself.

Mary was released back to her old unit, the Fifty-Second Ohio. She was immediately reassigned to proceed to Louisville, Kentucky, as a contract surgeon. She was scheduled to arrive just in time to be ordered to Atlanta, where General Sherman was forming preparations for a huge battle. From her experience she knew the General's "planning time" could mean several weeks or more.

She had hoped that her experiences to this date would have brought her a field commission as an officer, but it did not. For the most part, her captivity appeared to be ignored by the military. That hurt. She brushed away the thought, but nonetheless felt she was deserving of some type of recognition. It was, however, a time of confusion, uncertainty, and chaos among the Union's commanding officers.

Mary's next stop was getting back to Oswego and reuniting with her family. Just being back in friendly surroundings lifted her spirits. It was always good to feel the closeness of her family around her. Obviously, since she was still a free agent, she decided to give herself a furlough. A new plan was forming in her mind. She would go back home to the farm, rest a while, and then rent a room for a few days in Washington. There she could catch up on what was happening and maybe do a little lecturing. She could also campaign a little for Lincoln's reelection.

One strange event did happen. For her services from March to August, 1864, Mary received an unexpected payment of $432.36.

"Thank God. But does this payment mean I am at last a soldier?" She was left to wonder.

Within a few weeks she did receive acknowledgement as Acting Assistant Surgeon, United States Army. Along with it she was notified that she would be given a salary of one hundred dollars a month. She suspected she had Generals McCook and Thomas to thank for this. But she was still a contract surgeon, therefore a civilian soldier. She sent back her request to continue working on the battlefield. It was denied. Perhaps they felt she needed a rest. Deep in her heart, she agreed.

With a renewed spirit, it wasn't long before Mary was commuting back and forth. Soon, she began making the rounds of the lecture halls. Now she was able to talk first-hand about the war, while at the same time speaking out for President Abraham Lincoln's reelection. Her loyalty ran deep. She felt that she could now consider him a personal friend. It was also easier to forgive him for some of his earlier harsh words to her. She admired his stand, and felt deeply that she owed the President her strongest support.

For her entire life Mary had avidly followed the politics of the day. During the 1850s she had witnessed a political system that had been practically demolished. In 1856 the Republican Party put together its first ticket. Politicians who had fought one another, came together. Illinois Senator Abraham Lincoln, then a Whig, was favored as an 1860 candidate for President. Lincoln chose fellow Senator Hannibal Hamlin, a Democrat, as his partner for vice president.

They were opposites in many ways; Hamlin coming from a prosperous family and being well educated. But at the time Hamlin held a strong influence in the Senate. Lincoln recognized these qualities. Together they won!

Drawing upon his Senate background, Hamlin helped Lincoln build a strong Cabinet. His influence, however, began to weaken through the years. As the war went on, he was not consulted as often and considered himself to be a "fifth wheel," or was compared to Great Britain's royal family as a "spare" son, standing by in case he was needed. He did urge Lincoln to issue an Emancipation Proclamation and may have helped him write it.

Although Hamlin was willing to stand with Lincoln for reelection in 1864, Lincoln realized he needed a stronger candidate to join him on the ticket. He chose Tennessee Republican Governor Andrew Johnson. Dejected, Hamlin joined the Union Army as a corporal and went on to serve for several months.

Mary felt confident in Lincoln's choice. Through the fall, she attended many rallies, making it a point to talk about Lincoln's qualities and accomplishments. If she was up early walking around Washington, she often saw him out riding and gave him a wave. She admired him as anyone would a "peoples' champion."

Not one to be idle, Mary believed she was now ready to take on a new short-term assignment. She felt she had recuperated in both spirit and health. A location she had her eyes on was the Women's Prison in Louisville, Kentucky. Her friend, Dr. Edward Phelps, was the surgeon in charge of that region, if not the facility. He liked Mary and so favored her by giving her a good recommendation. Her next step was to apply.

Chapter 20

Off to Louisville

Mary didn't feel she would have any trouble. The General in command of that region was one she knew, William Tecumseh Sherman. She had heard so many good reports about him while back in Washington and that he had returned to the field. She decided her best way to contact him was to write him.

By now, Mary had learned a great deal about letter writing. She felt she had become a master at it since her school days. She had been told that only one in fifty letters would get to the person it was addressed to because all the politicians had dozens of staff people working for them. Gatekeepers, they were called. Still, she felt sure that a letter of this nature would go instead to the General's chief of staff, Edward Townsend. This time she was just going to ask for a specific posting rather than some vague position that very likely might hinge on a political appointment.

Another lesson Mary had learned was to do her homework. From what she had learned, she estimated that there were twenty-five to thirty female prisoners and refugee patients at the Prison. An ideal situation. So already she had decided how to handle this request.

What she wanted was to be named as a commissioned major, assigned to duty as a surgeon.

In her letter, Mary reminded the General that she had "already served the Government in a variety of ways" and that her performance had been commended and recognized by her medical colleagues. Mary's letter was explicit and complete.

General Sherman's staff agreed; it sounded like a good idea. Dr. Walker's reputation as a physician on the battlefield already preceded her. So, on October 5, 1864, Mary received her commission. She was officially awarded the contract as Acting Assistant Surgeon, U.S. Army. That meant more authority, and hopefully more income.

A request fulfilled

Now Mary was on her way to the Louisville Female Prison with one little change. The title meant "surgeon in charge."

But to Mary's surprise and total shock, the Prison turned out to have far more patients than reported—two hundred to three hundred. The current administrators immediately voiced their displeasure with the change. Mary hardly had time to unpack her bag or do an assessment of the Prison's problems before she was hit head on with them.

First of all, she was a female doctor, and that alone created resentment. No matter which way she turned, she was caught between two forces—administrative personnel and prisoners. Immediately she was faced with the fact that the financial situation at the prison was not good either. At times, as days went on, Mary even found herself paying from her own pocket for the laundry or the delivery of food just to get those situations resolved.

Although this was Union territory and Union authority,

the prisoners and patients in the Prison-Hospital were considered Confederates. In truth, many really were.

The Prison's administration was comprised primarily of medical staff, guards and superior officers. Many positions of authority were being held by personnel who had been there for long periods of time Mary had just come out of a poorly kept, disruptive, and destructive environment at Castle Thunder.

"I don't want any of those abuses reoccurring under my supervision," she declared.

Immediately, Mary was accused by both sides of being either too lenient or too harsh. One example that was emphasized was her failed effort to bring a unification to the facility. She was accused of playing favorites sometimes. During the Christmas season, Mary was accused of giving a group of Union patients little Union flags. That drew more complaints.

By January, Mary could see this assignment was not going to work out for her. She was spending valuable time writing letters to various doctors within the Army chain of command explaining her position. Nothing was going right. Letter writing wasn't working. Dispatches took too long to reach their destination and then a response took even longer to be returned.

Mary was being challenged at every turn. At last, she had taken too much. In March, she formally requested a transfer back to the battlefield. Once again, Mary's colleague Dr. Phelps came to her rescue by agreeing, perhaps recognizing that she did indeed need a slower pace.

Surprisingly, Mary's six month position at the Prison did meet with some approval from the *Louisville Daily Journal*. The newspaper reported on March 28, 1865 that they approved her stay there, considered her qualified for another assignment, and they wished her well.

On April 11, Mary was given charge of the Orphanage and Refuge Home located near the Red and Cumberland Rivers outside Clarksville, Tennessee. With good wishes ringing in her ears, Mary left Louisville. This time she had her old nemesis, Dr. George Cooper of the Army of the Cumberland to thank for quickly replacing her so she could be on her way within a few days. For her six month's assignment at the prison, she was paid $766.16. She was thirty-three years old.

Again, Mary was going to have an opportunity to work with refugees, many of them women and children. She felt it just had to be a much more pleasant experience. Perhaps this had been her calling all the time—to nurture others.

Chapter 21

The War Ends

Mary followed in the footsteps of her father as a devoted reader of newspapers, and particularly international publications. Perhaps that contributed to her being such a proficient letter writer. She could speedily write out a news item for a newspaper, and often did, offering opinion pieces that occasion-ally went to print.

On April 9, 1865, Robert E. Lee, General of the Army of Northern Virginia, surrendered to General Ulysses S. Grant, who was Commander of the Union Armies. They met in the McLean House in the village of Appomattox Court House, Virginia. Brief information came via telegraph, but more explicit details always followed in the newspapers.

Mary remembered that several days after reading about General Lee's surrender, she had also read an announcement about the President's activities. President Lincoln and his wife and General Grant and wife would be attending a play at Ford Theater called "*Our American Cousin.*"

These tidbits of news were intended to show people across the country that unity had returned, and that the times were returning to normal. The war was over. But even by the end of the war, President Lincoln, his Cabinet, and supporters had not formed a plan to reintegrate the seceded southern states back into the Union. The country had fallen into a state of indecision. In the South, the governors were being looked to for rebuilding instructions. In the West, the military represented much of the law.

All of the uncertainty and speculation that had begun as far back as the beginning of December 1863 was being described as a "period of reconstruction." Now, many new causes were requiring attention.

By the time that President Lincoln was to attend the play, the attendees had changed. By that evening, the Grants had pulled out and been replaced by Washington's Mayor Henry Rathbone and his fiancée, Clara Harris. The President and Mrs. Lincoln were rumored to be attending reluctantly.

A dreadful deed

Suddenly, by the next morning, the shocking news was being carried by telegraph around the world, and newspaper boys were hawking it from the street corners:

On April 14, 1865 at 9:30 p.m. Abraham Lincoln, President of the United States, was assassinated.

Mary read these unbelievable headlines in *The New York Times*. Every newspaper across the country had a similar headline across its front page:

President Lincoln Shot by an Assassin

The Deed Done at Ford's Theatre Last Night

The Act of a Desperate Rebel

The President Still Alive at Last Accounts.

No Hopes Entertained of His Recovery.

Attempted Assassination of Secretary Seward.

Official details

War Department, Washington April 15, 1:30 A.M. - Maj. Gen.Dis.

"This evening at about 9:30 P.M. at Ford's Theatre, the President, while sitting in his private box with Mrs. Lincoln, Mr. Harris, and Major Rathburn, was shot by an assassin, who suddenly entered the box and appeared behind the President.

The assassin then leaped upon the stage, brandishing a large dagger or knife, and made his escape in the rear of the theatre.

The pistol ball entered the back of the President's head and penetrated nearly through the head. The wound is mortal. The President has been insensible ever since it was inflicted, and is now dying."

Mary's hands trembled as she read the accounts. This was a shock that sent her falling to her knees as reality caught up with her; her obligation to her slain President, maybe even to her country, was gone. Death had surrounded her in many places, and now she was alone and more confused and frightened than ever.

She was invited to attend memorial services at a local Episcopal church. She attended wearing her surgeon's pants with the green stripe down the side, a major's epilates on her jacket, and her customary short skirt over pants.

Mary found herself becoming even more frequently depressed. She did not feel the passion and enthusiasm she once took pride in sharing. She had worked vigorously for Lincoln's reelection. She had admired his qualities as a leader. She remembered best the early mornings when she had seen him riding with his son as she had been out walking. That poor boy. She mourned for him in losing a father.

Most of all, Mary remembered the President's robust laughter, his off-color humor, the fact that he remembered her name and always greeted her heartily. She truly felt that he had appreciated her dedication. He was a man she could admire, and she was proud to have known him and his family.

She could not say the same for his successor, Andrew Johnson.

Mary didn't like Andrew Johnson's values. For one, he drank. Rumors were that he had been intoxicated at the time he took the oath of office as President. She thought, and later wrote: *"Everybody sees men who make and execute laws 'taking a little' and so if they ever expect to be great, they must follow in the steps of the illustrious."*

Chapter 22

Picking up the Pieces

On June 15, 1865, Mary's Army contract officially ended and she was released. She breathed a deep sigh of relief. It was done.

The summer came and went. The dreadful year, 1865, soon was coming to an end. Once again, Mary was heading back to Washington, still undecided what she would do. She did know that was where any action would occur—meaning a job opportunity of some kind. Her expectations of receiving another appointment from the military were bleak. But hopefully there might be an area where she could still practice medicine.

No one was talking about the war any more, nor women's rights. The slaves had been freed. "Hurrah," they said. Yet, there were questions

Was the Emancipation Proclamation being interpreted correctly? It was said it was being understood in different ways in different parts of the country. Rumors abounded.

Yes, people's interests were changing and moving on to other topics, particularly rebuilding, or "reconstruction," as it was called. Newspaper articles talked about expansions in the West. Names like "carpetbaggers" and "homesteaders" were mentioned.

Mary was not only seeing those changes, but feeling them. Her once fierce ambition to become a beacon for women was waning, perhaps it was even dying.

Now when Mary looked in the mirror, she saw a ghost of her former self. She had lost a great deal of weight at Castle Thunder and was not regaining it. Her self-diagnosis was that she was not normal in the sense of being her old self. She knew that for a while, at least, she could not operate, but she could continue with a physician's general duties, if she could find the patients.

Facing facts

It had been many months since her release from Castle Thunder but her health continued to decline. Sometimes she had nightmares that startled her awake. She had lost so much weight, and because she was petite, many people often mistook her for a child. Still, she ignored the symptoms.

Eventually, she was forced to consider her health issues. She realized that she was becoming easily depressed. She did not feel the passion and enthusiasm she once took pride in sharing. She continued to observe these "after battlefield" signs of fatigue and weariness in veteran soldiers as they returned home.

She recognized those same signs in her own self-diagnosis.

Fatigue had caught up with her. She told herself that while this illness continued, she could not trust herself to practice as a doctor. Her once fierce ambition to be a physician was definitely fading, too, as she tried to settle into her former Washington lifestyle. (Her self-diagnosis was what might later be labeled as post-traumatic stress disorder, or PTSD).

Also, her eyes had continued to give her problems, continuing to deteriorate since her imprisonment. She now began wearing wire-rimmed glasses to see correctly. In the mornings her legs felt stiff and aching, and beneath her breath she may have whispered a few short words of prayer or a curse.

An old problem

Mary also felt it was time that she took up another matter that was still rankling her: the amount of her retirement pension from the Army. By now, she had talked with many veterans and learned that there was not an exact set amount for retirement pay.

For her current military service, Mary would receive a pension of eight dollars and fifty cents per month. Not enough! Nurses were being paid twenty. She needed to be officially recognized for her rank of Major Surgeon, for which she should receive an equal pay of twenty dollars per month.

That was when she decided to make more inquiries. She would do the one thing she had found to be the most effective – write letters to everyone she knew in Washington.

Except this time, she knew more people. That included President Andrew Johnson, who had succeeded Lincoln upon his assassination. In fact, she decided she would try and speak directly to President Johnson. But she knew too that she would have to change her manner of approach and to soften her attitude toward him; difficult, as she still thought he was rotten. Besides, he was also having his own political problems and was engulfed in impeachment proceedings.

Little did Mary know what forces of fate she was unleashing. Suddenly, and without a real explanation, Mary Walker's life changed.

Chapter 23

Encounter with Destiny

In a moment it was over. Mary surely closed her eyes.

Secretary of War, General Edwin M. Stanton, on behalf of President Andrew Johnson, attached the ribbon clasp to Mary's chest. She looked down at the Medal of Honor and caught her breath. With a second motion General Stanton gently straightened the ribbon, stepped back and began to read a lengthy proclamation. His voice was deep and solemn as he read from the paper, each word resonating throughout the chamber.

"Dr. Mary Edwards Walker.....Whereas it appears from official reports that Dr. Mary E. Walker, a graduate of medicine, has rendered valuable service to the Government and her efforts have been earnest and untiring in a variety of ways, and that she was assigned to duty and served as an assistant surgeon in charge of female prisoners at Louisville, Ky. upon the recommendation of Major Generals Sherman and Thomas, and faithfully served as a contract surgeon in the service of the United States, and has devoted herself with much patriotic zeal to the sick and wounded soldiers, both in the field and hospitals, to the determent of her own health, and has also endured hardships as a prisoner of war four months in a

Southern prison while acting as a contract surgeon, and

Whereas by reason of her not being a commissioned offi-cer in the military service, a brevet or honorary rank cannot, under existing laws be conferred upon her, and

Whereas in the opinion of the President an honorable rec-ognition of her services and suffering should be made

It is ordered That a testimonial thereof be hereby made and given to the said Dr. Mary E. Walker, and that the usual medal of honor for meritorious service be given her.

Given under the hand in the city of Washington, D.C. this 11th day of November, A.D. 1865."

Mary looked down at the top of the medal, but she really could not see it. As the General kept reading, only half of the words actually reached her ears. She was thinking back about the events that had brought her to this day. Incidents from the War flashed through her mind; pain, despair, laughter, fear. She could hardly believe she was receiving the Medal of Honor!

It was January 27, 1866. Mary Edwards Walker had been invited to the Capitol to personally receive this honor from Andrew Johnson, President of the United States. But for some unexplained reason, today, it was General Stanton that was standing in front of her. She surmised that the President was off on some other type of important business. This was a phrase she was often hearing these days whenever she inquired about the new President.

Mary fully realized that she probably was called a "pest," as were many of the other suffragettes who badgered the President's office with requests. It was a new day and a new attitude!

Before the presentation Mary had not had an opportunity to see the medal. For the moment, she had to be content to look down upon it and feel its presence on her chest. It was a prestigious event that was suddenly propelling her into the pages of history.

When the presentation was over, Stanton handed Mary the parchment paper proclamation.

Congratulations began coming from all around her. People she did not even know wanted to shake her hand. Others wanted to reach out and touch the medal. Some just stared at it in admiration; most wondered at it. Mary could already see that it held something of an attraction. Maybe she did not fully understand herself why people were so attracted by it, but she did understand that it was creating some kind of mystique, and that she was becoming a part of it. It was that special! She touched her hand to it to reassure herself that it was still there.

It was not until hours later, when Mary was in the privacy of her room, that she gently held the ribbon and turned the medal so she could see its face.

A magnificent five-point star bearing a profile of Minerva formed the face of the medal, with a striped ribbon above it. It was beautiful and perfect in its design. She touched it and brought it up to press gently against her lips and then back against her heart. She felt her breath catch. Her heart was beating with excitement. She could now understand why people admired it.

From that moment, as Mary looked onto its surface, she knew this was meant to be—and that her destiny was now intertwined with this medal. She was overwhelmed with an instant obligation to wear it every day and protect it forever.

But she wanted to further research the full meaning of its design to appreciate it even more. Two figures appeared on the inverted five-point star: Discord and Minerva. Minerva was a goddess who represented both war and the ancient wisdom of the Athenian democracy.

On the medal, Minerva is defending herself with a shield of stars and stripes. In her other hand she holds an axe in a fasces, a collection of tightly bound sticks that, for the Romans, symbolized authority through unity and singularity of purpose. Her opponent, Discord, is armed only with serpents. It was a specular piece of jewelry. Later, she learned it had been designed by William Wilson & Sons, silversmiths of Philadelphia.

It was not long before Mary realized how fully she had become an overnight celebrity. She was also slowly coming to realize that the medal was a passport of sorts to her achieving the goals she had set for teaching others about the plight of women's rights. She wondered deeply if she should consider this her destiny?

An announcement appeared in the Washington newspapers. Congratulations continued coming from friends and strangers alike.

"You must have your photograph taken by Matthew Brady," several friends urged. "His photographs of war actions are being praised everywhere. This is a great honor you will want to remember."

Having her photograph taken by Brady appealed to Mary. He was the photographer that had outfitted portable darkrooms in horse drawn covered wagons called "What's-its" and taken them to battleground areas during the War. Brady had made a name for himself, and even President Lincoln had praised his work. After the war, he had opened a studio in Washington.

For Mary, this was a serious yet exciting decision. She

chose to wear her customary uniform, a form fitting long sleeved blouse that was buttoned down the front and extended below her waist. Her skirt beneath fell to below her knees. Under the skirt she wore her customary pants. On her breast she pinned the medal.

Brady approved of her choice, she later told friends. In a second pose she chose to wear a dark small hat with short feathers, with her hair pushed behind her ears.

The photographic technique also intrigued Mary. Brady used glass plates that were coated with light-sensitive solutions that were immediately exposed and processed before it could dry. He had trained other men to use this process and they had taken several hundred photographs of war related sites.

Rumors begin

Mary had barely received the award when rumors began to circulate about her merit for receiving it. It was also hinted in at least one news account that Dr. Mary Walker's medal had been presented to her as a method of smoothing her feathers after she had written several angry letters to President Johnson lobbying for the rank of major. The rank of major carried a higher pension.

She was said to have irritated the President so badly that he had appealed to Secretary of War Edwin M. Stanton to find some way to appease her. They agreed to recognize Dr. Mary Walker in some way for her medical services. Stanton did so by ordering that she be given one of the Medals of Honor. Gossip among the administration's staff lent credibility to the fact that Mary had pestered the President more than once for an acknowledgement of her war services.

One staffer was quoted as having overheard the President say directly to Stanton, "find some way to get her off my back."

Mary discredited those rumors when she heard them. She pointed to the fact that her commendation was dated November 11, 1865, before President Lincoln's death. She preferred another rumor that suggested that her name had actually been proposed by President Lincoln upon the recommendation of Generals William T. Sherman and George Thomas.

However, Lincoln had been assassinated before the final list of recipients had been compiled. That thought was a comforting memory to Mary. She was also comforted by the news that hundreds of other soldiers were receiving the medal as well.

In fact, upon inquiry, Mary learned that records of the time substantiated that before the medals were even cast, individuals were being considered to receive them. As the story went, the Congress, it seemed, had once proposed to President Lincoln that some type of a "certificate of merit" should be presented when a "private soldier" would distinguish himself in the service. Along with the certificate, an additional pay increase of two dollars per month would be awarded.

The Navy, it seemed, had also proposed to Congress on December 12, 1861, that a medal be created for naval acknowledgements. The Army responded in February 1862 in their bill to the Senate that a Medal of Honor be designed for their use. Lincoln had approved that as well.

All of this medal discussion and eventual debate had come about after it was pointed out by newspaper articles that European countries actively presented medals connected to wars. Queen Victoria had created the Victoria Cross.

Germany presented the Iron Cross. France had created several medals for different battles. Many Congressmen had begun asking questions about why the United States had not created a medal of some type.

Thus, on July 14,1862, after a year of squabbling, it was approved that 1,500 medals would be cast. The intent or purpose for giving the medal had become muddled. Some Congressmen felt it should be awarded for a specific act of bravery. Others looked upon it as a tool to boost morale and even enlistment in a demoralizing army. Also, because so much time had passed, President Johnson's staff urged that the medals be distributed as quickly as possible. Immediately, a variety of reasons became acceptable, ranging from actual military service, to recruitment, to acts of a political nature.

In the end, the American Society of Honor determined that seven soldiers at the Battle of Bull Run had performed actions that deserved Medal of Honor recognition. Other recipients were soldiers of the Twenty-seventh Maine Division for re-enlisting. It was noted that twenty-nine officers and enlisted men who had been assigned to accompany the body of President Lincoln to its final resting site in Illinois had also received medals.

Another recipient was western frontier hero William Cody, better known as "Buffalo Bill," for his scouting and other activities in the Indian campaigns. But only one of those receiving the medal was a woman: "a lady doctor named Mary Edwards Walker."

So, as far as Mary knew she was the only woman to be so honored. Perhaps she really was what one account called her: **"destiny's daughter**."

With all that information in mind, Mary considered

herself as being in good company. She chose to believe that sentiment. She was anxious. She felt that she had earned the right to now move on to whatever life might offer. She was ready to take the next step, whatever that might be.

Chapter 24

To Olde London Town

There had been a few undecided weeks following the medal presentation when Mary struggled to get back on course again. To more than one of her friends she appeared restless, uncertain, and sometimes depressed. She had not been welcomed back into the suffragists' ranks as graciously as she had hoped by some of her friends. Maybe they were envious of her medal. That thought felt like a knife thrust into her heart. She didn't care, she told herself. But she did care. However, she didn't let it show.

Perhaps this mood was what Dr. Susannah (Susan) Dodd noticed about Mary when next the two met. Mary and Susan had first become acquainted in 1864 while Mary was studying at the Hygeia Therapeutic College in New York. At that time, Susan Dodd had been a student, writer, and lecturer on hygiene. After finishing her medical degree, she had gone on to establish her own college of hygienic medicine in St. Louis, Missouri with her sister-in-law, also a doctor. Both doctors continued to teach the principles of Dr. J. Thall. Mary and Susan had not been particularly close then, but they had kept in contact. Their philosophies were similar and they had become comrades because both enjoyed wearing pants.

"We're going to Europe to attend a Social Science Congress," Susan announced. "Come with us. It's an international assembling of medical people and there will be exhibits from all over the world."

Susan Dodd and her husband, Andrew, were planning to attend the medical conference and then continue with a trip to Scotland to lookup Andrew's relatives. Andrew had also served in the Union Army, so he and Mary always found something to talk about.

"We're planning to leave in August." Whatever else she might have said convinced Mary that this would be just the tonic that could get her moving again!

The activities of the suffragists around Washington had become sluggish and monotonous. It would also give Mary new discussion points to add to her lectures.

From the beginning of their friendship, Mary and Susan had found confidence in one another. Their compatibility on so many topics made them ideal companions. They not only shared many healthcare philosophies, but both agreed on the hygienic attributes of wearing pants. In her own way, Dr. Dodd also shocked the prudish critics of her era as much as Mary did. But the existence of a husband and family life may have sheltered her from more severe criticism.

Traveling around Europe sounded wonderful. Beginning to plan months in advance would allow Mary to make contacts in London to lecture and tour medical facilities. But there was one major problem: How would she pay for her ship ticket, traveling, and hotel expenses while in England? After putting their heads together, the answer seemed to be "selling Mary's status as a person of interest."

It became a new challenge for Mary and her friends as

they began making inquiries. Again, this was a time for Mary to preserve.

This was a new goal that challenged her and bolstered her spirit.

Letters and personal contacts were made by Mary's friends with newspapers and European steamship lines The goal was aimed at convincing one of them that such a news worthy person—lecturer, medalist, and political advocate—should receive complimentary passage to Europe. She might even qualify to secure a position as a medical assistant for the voyage

Through their combined efforts of inquiries and contributions, passage was obtained on the *Caledonia* to Liverpool. Success! Mary breathed a sigh of relief. She was on her way.

The right time

Mary immediately set upon a writing campaign to denominational and social organizations in England such as the East London Temperance Association. Her plan was to try and organize a lecture tour by which she could finance her stay and travels.

She had already learned from her previous lecture exercises around Washington and New York that contributions could not be counted upon. So, she decided to set a lecture fee and had cards printed bearing her photograph. Organizations related to the temperance movement were her primary targets. Temperance was a topic that was as strong in Great Britain as it was in America.

The voyage across the Atlantic was anticipated to take eight or nine days. That would give Mary much needed time to think and rejuvenate. She had already decided that some of her time would be delegated to planning how she should continue her participation in the National Dress Reform Association.

She had been a member since her early days practicing in Rome, NY. Before leaving America, she had been elected the organization's president. Setting up a firm leadership program was of major concern to her. And, she also wanted to be able to include remarks about it in her conversations and talks during any European opportunities.

Upon their landing in Liverpool, Susan Dodd had pre-arranged for them to tour the Royal Liverpool Infirmary and hospital. She was particularly interested in learning more about the British hospital system. As she had already established her own clinic, she wanted to keep up with the latest in medical techniques.

Right from the beginning, Mary began making new friends and receiving invitations to visit other hospitals and talk with their staffs. This was an atmosphere in which she was outgoing and at ease. She was a personality that created curiosity. That would work for her.

The journey begins

The original purpose for their trip was to attend the annual meeting of the Society for the Promotion of Social Science. It was convening in the town of Manchester. Perhaps this meeting had been of greater interest to Susan, but Mary was welcomed to tag along and sit-in on many sessions.

Not only did their program interest Mary—but it served to introduce her to the medical group. It also identified her war contributions and her medal to an extended audience that did not know her, nor had they ever heard of her. Instantly, she became the "celebrity" package. As the week continued, Mary did not hold back but voiced her opinions and observations on one of their popular topics, the "Prevention of Infanticide."

Although Mary had never been considered to be a top-notch speaker, the audiences warmed to her, showing their respect and interest in her comments, especially her discussion of "Dress Reform." Her remarks were supported by her own wardrobe. Her varying outfits contributed to their interest in her. Reporters following the event found her a worthy news topic, and considerable news print was devoted to Mary's comments during the conference. She became a notable and quotable presenter, and glimpses of her enlivened the meeting.

By the time the week had passed and the Society's sessions were over, Dr. Mary Walker was well-known by Londoners, and maybe throughout all of England. Every day she was gathering new friends and admirers, and setting up lectures with their help.

From that point, Mary was pretty much on her own. Although she had traveled with the Dodds, their plans were that they would travel around Glasgow, Scotland and northern England to visit Andrew's relatives. Mary would travel a different route, keeping in touch with them through short notes mailed back and forth.

Like her father, Mary was a serious reader. One book that seemed to have stuck with her more prominently than others was the writings of a French historian named Louis de Beaufort. One of the things he proclaimed was that "the future of society is in the hands of mothers." To this Mary responded proudly, paraphrasing an ending of her own:

"The future of society is in the hands of women."

Many of the comments from her various meetings Mary captured in notes with the thought that she might write a book upon her return home from London. Her enthusiasm had bounced back; she felt alive again. For a short time, she even employed an agent to arrange a few speaking dates but they soon quarreled over collecting fees.

Much of the time, Mary often relied upon her new acquaintances to evaluate her talks and how she might improve or enliven them. She was also beginning to clip newspaper articles from the British newspapers about women there who were contributing to the community. She felt these examples would make good references to add to her lectures.

New opportunities

What a charming creature! The petite unpretentious lady wearing the hand-tailored "Reform Dress" had literally swept across the sea from America. She was, they agreed, just as friendly and bright as someone might have imagined an American to be. She was soon circulating among the medical profession, as well as pursuing speaking engagements with the temperance groups in and around London.

Mary Walker's views were fresh and spontaneous and the somber English medical society applauded her frankness. She had met the challenge of becoming a woman doctor, practiced on the battlefields of the American War, and had been awarded a prestigious Medal of Honor that she wore every day on her breast. She also carried with her a copy of the Citation, just in case someone had doubts.

Mingling with this intellectual group was just the tonic Mary needed. In turn, they showed their respect and appreciation by inviting her into their homes and introducing her to their friends, colleagues, and patients. Mary was now so glad she had decided to come.

A royal visit

One of the opportunities that unexpectedly became available was visiting the English parliament. It was also a custom for anyone of note who traveled to London to request an audience with the Queen. Generally, this event was reserved for government officials, politicians, wealthy visitors, and prominent business persons. Mary's party placed requests.

If Mary at times doubted the prestige her presence carried, she never allowed it to show. But it had to be a great moment of sheer joy to her when a courier from the Court of St. James delivered an invitation for her to visit the Court. It was assumed that the Prince of Wales would do the honors, as Queen Victoria had been in a lengthy mourning period and was not performing public duties.

Not meeting the Queen was surely a disappointment. When reading about the Queen's marriage, Mary had been deeply impressed by the devotion of the Queen and her husband, Prince Albert. On more than one occasion, Mary had expressed the thought that:

"There should be perfect freedom for women to select a partner for life in a straight forward, honest, and honorable manner."

The first question in Mary's mind was about what she should wear. It was also said that the atmosphere surrounding the Court was not one of flamboyance. Finally, she decided to wear something somber, similar to what she had worn for her photograph. Fortunately, she had brought along that same little black straw hat. She remembered that Matthew Brady had complimented her on her choice.

However, when Mary reached the Court, rumors were spreading that the Queen was there and would be meeting everyone in the guest line. And she did.

Whatever words Queen Victoria and Mary exchanged remained private. But it was another experience she hoped to share only with her family. She was also given a shawl, it was reported.

Yes, things were going well. Another stand out event for Mary was fulfilling her contract to speak at St. James Hall in London on February 26, 1867. She would remember it always.

Some critics

Up to this time, several of the lectures on Mary's schedule had been arranged by the London Temperance League and usually held in area churches where meeting rooms were small, as was the audience. The St. James Hall was large, with a capacity for an audience of three hundred.

As was her habit, Mary wrote out her lectures on sheets of paper and read from them, as to keep on track, although she could venture off them to answer question or add remarks.

That particular day, a group of medical students came to hear her and were seated in the balcony. As she moved along with her talk, they began to heckle her with catcalls. They were finally silenced, but thereafter she felt more secure speaking in smaller halls.

Another memorable lecture was given at Dunham Town Hall. Seated in the audience was a newspaper reporter who filed a story mentioning that she had read from a manuscript in present- ing an hour-and-a-half talk.

"She spoke briefly about her imprisonment at Castle Thunder. She told of her sleeping on a pest infested mattress. the lack of good food and that she was proud to have been traded for a Southern officer physician."

The reporter went to detail describing what Mary wore as

"a black cloth tunic that came to her knees, with gimpy trimming down the front and border, worn over pantalettes of the same material." To it was pinned an honor medal. He called the audience somber.

At the time Mary pretty much ignored such remarks. Alone, in private, she probably stomped her foot or pounded her fist against a desk. Anyway, she considered it a success.

Chapter 25

On to Paris

"Come with us, Mary, to Paris," invited her new acquaintances. "It's the World Exposition! You'll have a great time."

In planning her trip to London, Mary had not even thought about going to Paris. But now it seemed to be a "have to go" trip as it was so close. She had already heard and read a great deal about the *Universelle Exposition*, or world's fair, that had opened in Paris in April and was still going on. Hundreds of Americans were flocking over to view the exposition which was said to be even more extravagant than the previous British Expo.

Mary had read that the American government had entered many exhibits and received over 200 medals and citations in several categories. Surely one exhibit of considerable interest to Mary was of military medical equipment that had received a gold medal. She was also familiar with other American medal recipients: the McCormick reaper, Walter Wood's mowing machine, Elias Howe's sewing machine, and C. F. Chickeling's pianos.

How glorious! Mary was filled with pride and admiration. She agreed with the general sentiment that America's government was now taking the world seriously and wanted to show off their products and capabilities.

In anticipation of a great day, Mary caught a surrey from her hotel to the Exposition gate, where masses of people were already gathering, standing in line to buy tickets. There were visitors from all over the world dressed in their native wardrobes. She realized she would hardly be recognized. As she walked through the gates into a fairyland park, excitement began to build in her and all the surrounding visitors. There were gasps of wonder and cheers.

It was the beginning of a spectacular visit.

The park had been designed with miles of narrow streets. On either side they were lined with elegant restaurants and large building displays. The park encircled the main exhibit amphitheater, where other exhibits were also on display. Each one seemed to be more interesting and informative than the previous. Visitors could stroll through a Tunisian Palace or a Catholic Cathedral. There also stood an award-winning, rustic American one-room school house that expressed "the freedom of education for everyone." It had received a Chavalieis of the Imperial Order, one of the highest awards.

Seeing all of these exhibits in the park and in the exhibit hall was exhausting but exhilarating for Mary. Her spirits were high. She was glad she was wearing sturdy shoes. It was no wonder that she carried that exuberance into her next event—a Fourth of July celebration being hosted for all the Americans in Paris.

Again, what should she wear? She knew it would be a fun time. She quickly prepared a red, white, and blue sash to wear either around her waist or over her shoulders.

It was held at the Grand Hotel. A large contingent of

Americans came, distinguished and ordinary, government officials, politicians, business people, soldiers. It was a mixture of Americans from everywhere, even those living in Paris. Speech after speech was given from a raised stage and podium set up at the head of a room filled with tables. It was loud, it was jubilant, it was a wildly celebratory atmosphere!

Mary was seated among this loud, boisterous crowd; some singing, others drinking wine and giving toasts between the different speakers. Everyone knew she was a teetotaler, but she was enjoying the comradery. One speaker followed another. For Mary, it all suddenly became repetitious and boring. Spontaneously, she rose from her seat and began jauntily walking toward the stage.

Surprised, the speaker stopped. Mary stepped up on the riser and raised her glass. She loudly shouted out a toast declaring "here's to the soldiers and sailors."

Dramatically, she reached out to an American flag on a standard nearby and lifted its edge to her lips. The hall burst into a spontaneous cheer. Solemnly, Mary walked back to her seat, totally astounded by her behavior.

By the next morning the French newspapers had sent back a story to the American press. Whether Mary felt a sense of remorse or embarrassment she didn't let it show. While in Paris she had also planned to visit hospitals, and so she went about planning for that.

She realized that many sources might consider her spontaneous actions one of an exuberant, perhaps crazy, woman. She hoped they would not. It was time to go back to London.

There the Dodds had decided it was time for them to return home. But Mary still had a few speaking obligations to fulfill. She also wanted to think. It had occurred to her during her stay that she could continue living in Britain. She had found success there with her lectures, giving over thirty in her year's stay .

Mary may have recalled, too, that the Blackwell Sisters had been forced to flee to England to be able to practice medicine. Possibly, she could continue her profession there. In the end, she decided it was time to return to Washington. Her mission was still not completed.

It was August. Once home there would still be time to do a lecture tour before winter came.

Chapter 26

Back Home

Mary's observation of Washington City was that it had become highly political—and expensive to live there. Only a handful of her friends remained. Yet she persevered. There were days when she stood on the same steps to the Patent Office that she had stood on when she first came to Washington. It had now been renamed the Indiana Hospital. Except now the mud was gone, the blood spots had been removed, and everywhere, everyone wanted to forget the war.

Susan Anthony, Belva Lockwood and the remainder of suffragists had now banded together to take up the last remaining question. What was their cause now? Were they still determined to win the right to vote?

Getting the vote did not excite Mary, as she had always considered herself free. But she did recognize even stronger that Washington was the center where business connections were being made. Here was where the influence for the entire nation had gathered. So, she volunteered once again. Resilience had become a part of her nature.

Mary hung out her medical sign once again and began planning another lecture schedule. She knew she would attract only a handful of patients, but she could concentrate on writing more articles. Perhaps, this was even the time to write that book she had long hoped to publish.

Condemning tobacco

Yes, Mary was excited to be back in Washington City. She was certain this was the place where she could be the most influential, particularly on women's issues. But there was also one negative factor she could not suppress: Tobacco!

The use of tobacco was rapidly spreading in popularity across the country. Mary considered cigars the worst! They appeared to be th signature choice of influential politicians and businessmen of all varieties. Pipe smoking, cigarettes, and chewing tobacco were growing in popularity, particularly among younger people. Many offices were so filled with smoke Mary felt like she was walking through a cloud. And, the odor carried throughout a building. Spittoons lined the hallways, with every office sporting at least one.

But too often, Mary had to avoid any confrontation on the topic with those men she wished to talk with or meet. She taught herself to hold her tongue. On the other hand, it became a strong topic she had begun to emphasize in her lectures. She was convinced that tobacco was harmful to one's health and could create marital complications.

She also made it a point to collect facts and anecdotes about tobacco that she could include in her lectures. These were also facts she still hoped to include in a book one day.

"**Wasted in Smoke**—It is estimated that 20,000 cigars are daily sold on Broadway, New York, of which one-twentieth cost 30 cents, two twentieths 25 cents, one fifth 20 cents, two fifths 15 cents, and one fourth 10 cents; making $3,300 a day, or $1, 204,500 a year for cigars on that single street. It is also estimated that 75,000,000 cigars are consumed in the city at a cost of $9,650,000. This, with the amount annually expended for pipes and tobacco, makes an aggregate of $10,500,000 yearly consumed in smoke in this city."

She was quick to point out that "if this ten-thousand dollars were expended in providing homes and food for the worthy poor, and unfortunately degraded women of New York, thousands of agonies would be relieved and millions more prevented. ..."

By now, Mary's emotions had run the gamut from highs, to depression, to exasperation, to patience. It was difficult to hide, or even disguise, how strongly she felt toward certain suffragists. There were many causes in which she felt they could be involved. Yet, she forced herself to be amenable, recognizing that she was dependent upon their acceptance.

Chapter 27

Meeting Challenges

Mary Walker's contemporaries of the time were a handful of tough, determined, and experienced women who took pride in being called Suffragettes—women seeking equal rights, or Sisters, as they called one another.

Some of the time they were now wearing white dresses to emphasize who they were. Some of them lived in or around Washington, while others traveled there from their homes in other states to lecture or lobby government officials. Many shared similar backgrounds with Mary, growing up in rural areas, teaching school as a teenager while striving to reach a personal goal. Like Mary, they recognized Washington as the center of government power.

As a teenager, Mary had grown up hearing and reading about some of these women and admiring their activities. By now she knew most of them personally, or by sight or reputation. The most active of them at the end of the war included Susan B. Anthony, Elizabeth Cady Stanton, Lucy Stone, Victoria Woodhull, and Belva Lockwood. They headquartered and planned their activities out of the Central Women's Suffrage Bureau. Although Oswego was only a train ride away, Mary was resolute about staying in Washington. She recognized that the Capitol was where change could be influenced. She felt confident her opinions could make a difference, but she did admit that she was a "Maverick."

Yes. She realized that characteristic in herself. She admitted she didn't get along smoothly with some of the other suffragettes, but she also felt strongly that she had been able to draw attention to the cause through some of her antics. She had come to realize that often her confrontations with police drew the very attention their crusade needed. It would be mentioned in a newspaper at times when it ordinarily might not have. It was not a lady-like approach that brought approval from her acquaintances, but it worked. There were a few who even considered it the early stages of marketing.

Edward W. Nye of the New York *World* newspaper had become well known for his cartoon treatment of the war. Because of her dress and antics, Mary became a favorite subject for him and he labeled her "a self-made man." He persisted in cartooning her. It was difficult for Mary to ignore such publicity. But she did.

Fortunately, she had learned to bite her tongue rather than rub a Sister the wrong way. She also knew very well that her appearance and insistence on wearing pants embarrassed many of them, but she was not about to change or give up her freedom of dress. Up to now, in every lecture, she continued to forcibly claim that it was her *"right to dress as [she] please in free America on whose tented fields [she] have served four years in the cause of human freedom."*

Such statements quickly drew harsh criticism from Susan Anthony. Upon occasion, Anthony's sharp tongue had already criticized other Sisters for having too many children or not working diligently enough for their cause. On other occasions,

Anthony had glared at Mary or brushed her aside at lectures. She had not confronted her face to face, but Mary knew that one day she would.

A dreary job

There was nothing glamorous about being a suffragist. It was drudge and dreary work. There was nothing exciting about getting up early in the morning, lacing up sturdy high buttoned shoes, and slogging through wind, rain, or snow along Washington's streets to rally at the Capitol or outside other buildings. It took genuine dedication and perseverance.

In her own mind, Mary Edwards Walker considered herself free. She had always felt free to do as she pleased and did not feel that a new law by the Government would give her more freedom. But she also recognized that a majority of women were timid to this idea and were willing to wait until officially freed by the government—whenever that might be.

Tough ladies

While Mary had been growing up in Oswego, teaching and going to medical school, Susan Brownell Anthony had been starting her career. Susan Anthony was a Quaker, or a member of the Friends Society, as some called them. Their religious doctrine already considered men and women to be equals. She grew up around Rochester, New York, and had started teaching school at age seventeen. After ten years of teaching, she longed to do something more satisfying, but teaching was the only recognized profession for women.

She therefore began crusading with local temperance groups against the use of alcohol. As her interest in the subject grew, she then established a group of her own called The Daughters of Temperance. Recognizing that she needed a broader field of reform, Anthony started traveling to Washington and other nearby cities, going door to door handing out pamphlets and getting petitions signed.

She also began writing temperance articles for a newspaper called *The Lily* that was owned by a woman named Amelia Bloomer.

Like Anthony, Bloomer was also a woman of strong opinions. She was interested in equal rights for women and participated in area rallies and parades. Anthony encouraged women to form unions. She also lectured for emancipation, but felt black men should not be given the right to vote ahead of women.

Another long-time worker in the suffragist movement was Elizabeth Cady Stanton, whom Mary had read about and admired for years.

Co-crusaders' history

Elizabeth Stanton and Susan B. Anthony had known each other for years, going to the same rallies and partnering on projects. In 1848, they organized the Equal Rights convention that was held in Seneca Falls, New York. It was a historic event that anyone interested in equal rights discussed many times.

"She had a generous nature and a depth of tenderness that few women possessed," friends said about Elizabeth. This was the opposite of how Anthony was described.

These two then, Anthony and Stanton, appeared to be the stalwarts of the Washington Women's Bureau. Although both were dedicated, Mary considered Susan Anthony to be the stronger politician, with much of the credit and publicity seeming to go her way.

There was no doubt that Elizabeth Stanton held to her

own views on certain topics, such as her famous omission of the "obey pledge" from her wedding ceremony to abolitionist leader Henry B. Stanton.

That alone had made her popular with many women. She further believed that women should not submerge their personal identity when they married. So, working together, their dedicated but resolute feminine ways helped them to achieve the popularity and monetary support they needed to keep their ambitions alive.

Lucy Stone was another member of the old group. She had been the first Massachusetts woman to earn a college degree, and many felt that gave her a good standing among the suffragists. She kept busy, working more in the East and cultivating support groups than coming into Washington.

Yet another Sister that Mary related to very well was Belva Ann Bennett McNall Lockwood, who was acknowledged to be one of the first women lawyers in America. They had formed a friendship quickly upon Mary's arrival in the Capitol and shared many similarities. Both had grown up in New York State, taught school as teenagers, and Belva at one time had taught school and worked in and around Oswego.

Belva's first husband, Urich McNall, had been a farmer and died of consumption. She had married at eighteen and widowed at twenty-three. They had a daughter named Laura. Her second husband, Ezekiel Lockwood, had been a war veteran, Baptist minister, and practicing dentist who held progressive ideas about women's rights. He particularly supported Belva's pursuit of studying the law. They had a daughter named Allison.

Mary liked Lockwood's demeanor and philosophy, so much so that she decided to rent a room from her at her

Washington address on F Street. It was an old, twenty-room house that Belva had bought upon the death of her second husband as a means of supporting herself and her family. She had converted the rooms into her law office, living quarters for her family, and extra rooms for renting out for fifteen dollars a month. As their friendship grew, Mary may have considered Belva more of a mentor than a critic.

An extended family

Mary had also begun studying the law herself. She did not aspire to become a lawyer, but she had discovered that many of the poorer patients she treated had never heard of the simple legal laws that they might use to regain property or apply for a pension. Mary was particularly interested in understanding the Constitution.

Belva had studied the law and practiced it in Washington, even being one of the first women to present before the U.S. Supreme Court. One of her noteworthy acts had been to lobby for the first black attorney to present before the Court.

Both Belva and Mary shared a preference for wearing pants under their dresses. Belva wore pants frequently, except in the court room, where she feared her choice of dress would cause prejudice. Both had tried wearing the "Bloomer style" and dismissed it.

As close friends, both women campaigned as suffragists, marching in rallies, and loudly voicing their opinions. In fact, Belva, her daughters, a niece Clara Bennett, and other young women who boarded with the Lockwood's, apparently enjoyed running off together to join the various rallies that gathered and marched around Washington City.

Increasingly often the ladies would dress in white dresses

so that they resembled a flock of white swans skipping along the streets, shouting out their slogans and enjoying their camaraderie.

Holidays were an especially good time for these groups to gather, often being joined by out-of-state Sisters, or traveling to cities where nearby rallies took place. Mary enjoyed this family like relationship, and admired Belva and her family greatly.

One of the best parades of the year was held in Washington on the Fourth of July, and was followed by fireworks. Here, the Suffragists could really express their cause with a meaningful parade.

There was a difference between parades and rallies. Parades were organized with a formal appearance. The ladies often marched four abreast, standing tall with many proudly carrying home-made signage. Sponsors joined them in decorated wagons or with bands. Rallies were more informal, just boisterous gatherings, with men and women walking along together, sometimes arm in arm with lots of shouted out slogans and maybe songs. Both served their purpose.

Mary appeared to particularly enjoy these rallies, frequently shouting at policemen who threatened to arrest her for wearing men's attire.

As the years of such rallying went on, Mary added to her wardrobe. She liked a vest and wore different small, lace-trimmed, white neck scarfs, which were in style. She also wore a mink cape over her coat depending on the season. It was reported that once, for a special occasion, she even made a white vest, pants, and frock coat. To add drama, she wore white gloves. She liked to dress for the occasion, depending on the season and the importance of the event or the persons involved.

Frequently, she carried a folded black umbrella, using it like a cane and swinging it along. And, of course, using it when it rained.

In contrast to the other suffragists in white dresses, Mary Walker stood out shockingly. Yes, she drew complaints from her friends for making a spectacle of herself. That spectacle often turned into a cartoon sketch by Nye or a line or two of copy in a local newspaper. The contrast was even greater in newspaper photographs when she joined other suffragists who were wearing fashionable wide brimmed hats with multiple flowers around the brim.

Mary brushed the criticism aside. She was convinced it brought attention to their cause. She felt that in this way she was becoming a publicist for the cause. It did bring criticism even from close friends like Belva but at the time did not damage their relationship

During those years, one man named Fredrick Douglas had become a strong leader in the women's movement. Born a slave, he had escaped from Baltimore, Maryland, in1838 to New York City. He was well educated, and had become a strong orator and writer opposing slavery. From the mid-40s to 1847, he had toured and lived in Europe, becoming well known there before returning to the Washington area.

Douglas had been active in the women's suffrage movement as far back as the Seneca Falls Convention and had been the only black man there. He had founded and edited the *North Star* newspaper and was a leader of the Colored National Party, as well as later becoming affiliated with the Equal Rights Party formed after the Civil War by another active suffragist, Victoria Woodhall.

Among the quotations that Douglas frequently included in his speeches was the statement, "We are American citizens; by the principles of the Declaration of Independence, we are American citizens the of the U.S. Constitution we are American citizens…."

Mary Walker was among the suffragists who joined Douglas in several rallies and at times helped him organize others.

Chapter 28

Sisters Apart

Mary gave serious attention to the women that surrounded her. She could see that most of the Sisters were entrenched in their personal pursuits. Out of all the activities that were happening around Washington and gaining the most publicity, Mary decided to pursue three goals: dress reform, hygiene, and the right of women to vote.

She had already learned that sometimes these movements marched hand-in-hand with her goals and at other times they did not. She knew this would require continued discipline and would occupy a great amount of her time. But she was convinced that she had both the discipline and the time to tackle them. What else was she up against in pursuing these goals? Immediately she knew the answer: Money!

One of the first projects Mary knew she could assist with was helping Susan B. Anthony and Lucy Stone organize the Women's Suffrage Association for Ohio.

She also began coordinating more activities for the Central Women's Suffrage Bureau in Washington. This was a responsibility that Mary knew well and had already shown her success in coordinating volunteers to help in such social events. The other Sisters recognized that Mary had a talent for doing these time-consuming projects and invited her to work on their campaigns as well.

Hours of meetings and hundreds of letters and flyers needed to be written as part of every campaign. Mary quickly set those tasks in motion. She had always been good at persuading other women to become volunteers. These were all small paying jobs—but, enough to keep her going.

These activities continued to prove to Mary that there was nothing self-satisfying about being a suffragist. By September, Mary's projects were completed, so she handed off the day-to-day operations to other members and volunteers. She had frugally saved her earnings. She decided it definitely was time for a change.

But what? Maybe it was time for her own lecture tour?

Two halls that she frequently attended, either listening to Sisters or lecturing herself, were the Union League Hall on Ninth Street in downtown Washington or the Odd Fellow's Hall on Seventh Street. She probably favored the Odd Fellows Hall because it had already become the largest and most popular venue. It promised a larger contribution when she spoke there.

This particular Hall offered what the *Evening Star* called a "fascinating glimpse" into the future. Lectures were but a small part of their offerings. The three-story building hosted art exhibits, play performances and panoramas, fancy dinners, and weekly dances. Its elaborate façade whetted the imagination and drew in the elite and well-dressed residents of the city and beyond. Rows of polished wooden benches with carved back railings offered comfortable seating beneath handsome gas lights.

During this time, Mary had also put together her position

paper on hygiene and added new touches to her long-standing Reform Undergarment paper. She now felt she had the time and a strong program to offer.

Mary believed her comments made good copy for the local publications. She was well-read in the politics of the day, both nationally and locally. She talked to many of the elite every day around the Capitol and freely expressed her opinions on just about every problem that arose.

However, she was sad that many of her Sisters disagreed with her on some of the current issues. They were often embarrassed by her spontaneous criticism of a politician or a legislative decision that frequently popped up in the newspapers.

Homemade Dresses

This was a time when thousands of women made their family's clothing, as well as mending by patching them with swatches of new material. Mary was a home-schooled seamstress who had spent a lot of time restyling and tailoring her own garments and uniforms to suit her whims. The clothing she made was a testimony to her proficiency.

She had started out with a slightly fitted princess style skirt worn over a pair of pants. Over time, the dress had evolved into a blouse. Earlier, as a young woman, Mary, her mother, and sisters had experimented with Bloomer style costumes, rejecting them. Her father, Alvah Walker, also condemned corsets for cutting off the flow of oxygen and blood circulation in the body's midsection. He called them "steel torture instruments."

At one point, even Mrs. Bloomer had stopped wearing pants and made another fashion splash by advocating the wearing of hooped skirts that gave the illusion of a handsspan waistline. For a few years that style was considered to be fashionable by some, even though it was supported by billowing petticoats that weighed up to twelve pounds.

Mary was still content to continue wearing variations of her vests, pants and long coats. They provided the warmth needed for the inclement weather of the New England coast, but in particular for when Mary traveled in New York and Washington City.

Chapter 29

Confusing Times

The Eastern regional newspapers had carried back accounts of Mary's reception in England, particularly her audience with Queen Victoria. There had also been a dramatic account of her dedication in France as quoted by American observers at the dinner. She had become newsworthy again. Invitations to speak about her journey before temperance and political groups picked up around Washington City and New York.

The old celebrity feelings that fueled Mary's enthusiasm began to return. To her, it meant one thing—listeners and, hopefully, contributors. She knew, too, that the women who would hear her would be secretly hoping that she would be so bold as to wear her sash of Stripes. Yes, many looked forward to seeing her make a spectacle of herself. It would be worth it, she reasoned, if it helped move the cause for women's rights, dress reform, and temperance forward.

The months, then the years, moved on. The seasons changed. During that time (March 1861) Mary and Albert separated. Five years later a divorce was granted by State of New York. The Presidents changed: Ulysses S. Grant became president from 1869 to 1877. Mary didn't like him. He smoked cigars and always seemed to be surrounded by a rough crowd.

True or not, it was said that he was hiring or appointing many of his relatives to government jobs.

Still, the suffragists' efforts continued. Groups of them in different towns across the country had begun working together again, as they recognized their common goal was women's rights—and primarily, equality.

To many women, the issues had become confusing. At one point, there had been two women's suffrage organizations. The American Women Suffrage Association (AWSA) had been started by Lucy Stone and Julia Ward. They had petitioned the Congress to allow the women of Washington D.C. to vote and hold office. That failed.

Later in 1871, The National Women's Suffrage Association (NWSA) was founded by Susan B. Anthony and Elizabeth Cody Stanton. They petitioned Congress to extend suffrage rights to women and to allow them to speak on the floor of Congress. That failed too. Although strongly competitive, the groups consolidated, extending their efforts to include other social issues.

Principally, the leader was still Susan B. Anthony, and they headquartered in the Central Women's Suffrage Bureau. From there, they continued to coordinate programs, rallies, and campaigns with State suffragists' organizations. For much of the decade, it was difficult to add any excitement to their movement.

Mary united with the National Woman's Suffrage group in addition to hanging out her medical shingle on a house she rented. Again, women and children were her principal patients and they often turned into house guests. She kept busy. There were plenty of different causes circulating to ignite her interest, both locally and nationally.

By this time, Susan Anthony and Lucy Stone had parted over their philosophies. Lucy had married and had a daughter, and she wanted to spend more time at home with husband and family and less time campaigning. That was something of a traitorous act to the cause, in Susan's opinion.

Mary, who already considered herself emancipated, had little thought to direct toward gaining the right to vote. For that reason, many of her friends and acquaintances criticized her "maverick-like spirit."

Yes, Mary had done a lot of thinking while she lived in London. Her stronger interests now appeared to be toward dress reform, the practice of hygiene, and the use of tobacco and alcohol. As an aside, her insistence on wearing masculine-styled clothing often drew her away from the main reform cause.

Indeed, perhaps it was time for her to break away from the central core. She wondered if she could regain any of the momentum she had gotten from her European tour? Would any of her experiences appeal to Midwesterners? Yes, she decided. She had to reinvent or recharge herself.

Mary began enthusiastically setting up a lecture tour through the state suffragists' groups, where she would be talking about her experiences in London, Paris, and of course, profiling her Medal of Honor. Train transportation afforded Mary the luxury of traveling through New England and New York, then on to Ohio, Kansas, and Missouri. Suffragists' groups along the way were expected to recommend or help out with lodging and local transportation. Unfortunately, Mary's enthusiasm was dashed. It was disappointing in most places to only have small audiences as well as meager donations. She thought she had a story to tell. Now, she wondered at the wisdom of her plan. She enjoyed the travel and seeing other parts of the country, but it was becoming costly!

One high point came in Kansas City when she was arrested and immediately released, mostly for newspaper publicity purposes. Of course, it was about her wearing pants. But it did breathe life into her trip. Doggedly, Mary persisted, traveling into the South, stopping at Vicksburg and Jackson, Mississippi, then on to New Orleans and up to Austin, Texas.

Wearily, she returned to Washington with most of her savings gone. Her travels had taken about ten months. Not one to look back, she immediately set her sights on picking up where she had left off with her emphasis on dress reform and women's rights. Except now she could add a new theme and concentrate on Washington City's push for home-rule.

The Central Women's Suffrage Bureau again became one of her venues for lecturing. But now she was right back where she had started.

Reform dress

Dress reform had become one of Mary's lifelong pursuits, beginning with her youthful experimentations and continuing as she learned more about the reforms taking place in other parts of the world. She had learned a great deal about women in other countries, their personal habits, their marriage customs, and what they were wearing. She liked including these descriptions in her lectures. She discovered that American women were fascinated by the cultures of other women—not just that they wore pantaloons in India.

The dress reformers of the 1870s concentrated on reforming the undergarments, rather than trying to change the fashion of the outer dress. The bustle was not considered hazardous, so it was allowed to be an acceptable part of reform dresses. Reformers urged replacing the corset with a "waist," a short sleeved, high-necked garment that supported the upper body. It also had buttons on its lower edges, so that one might button one's petticoats to it, thereby using the shoulders to support the weight of the skirts. These outfits allowed greater freedom of movement and were sometimes called "Emancipation Waists."

Mary's goal was to achieve a *"perfect freedom of motion."* But she conceded that that was not always possible. For instance, elastic garters cut off circulation.

For reformers such as Mary, the tight necklines cut off breathing naturally and reduced circulation. However, this new reform in undergarments did not solve all the problem associated with fashion.

Other interests

Another of Mary's strong interests was her compassion and deep feelings for the women and children who still came wandering into Washington looking for displaced veterans or relatives. Many of them had no place to stay, nor money to pay for lodging. Many were found sleeping outdoors in foul weather, just as the soldiers had done when Mary had first come to the city. Her soft heart toward their problems kept her welcoming strangers into her home. Her hope was that they would share or contribute in some way to helping her maintain the home. That sentiment seldom worked out.

One newsworthy issue that came about was the founding of a new organization called the Women's Christian Temperance Union. Two long time temperance advocates, Frances Willard and Annie Turner, had organized this group in December 1873 in Hillsboro, Ohio.

They, too, considered themselves suffragists and urged women to support themselves by taking jobs outside the home and managing their own affairs. For many people, these causes seemed to be strange allies. But the opponent of both was the strong alcohol manufacturing industry that was rooted in the East and lobbied strongly in Washington. Mary agreed with their philosophy, but did not actively join this group.

For much of the decade, Mary Walker spent her days lobbying and lecturing in Washington for not only her personal causes, but other local social issues that arose. As Washington grew, suffragists circulated petitions on issues such as road repair, improved housing, and feeding the poor. Still, each day resembled the day before and the one following. Some progress had been made, but a greater interest seemed to be going elsewhere, particularly to the West.

One interesting point about spending the day at the Capitol was that constituents could eat in the House of Representatives dining room, or refectory, as it was often called. Occasionally, a congressman or lobbyist might invite a suffragist to his table if he was seeking reelection or support for his bill.

The food was prepared by local restauranteurs and brought in. The menu offered such dishes as beefsteak, oysters, seafood, or European cuisine. The prices were considered to be high. The dining room also offered considerable tobacco smoke and spirits. There was a Senate Dining Room offering similar foods.

Most suffragists working the Capitol packed a sandwich and ate it while sitting out on the Capitol steps, weather permitting. Street peddlers offered less expensive food and drinks, accompanied by fresh air.

During this same time period, suffragists in other states were working in their own communities to achieve equal rights.

Out west in the Wyoming Territory, women were campaigning in their own way. Unexpectedly, a woman's suffrage bill had been proposed there, and the male leadership of the territory agreed. There were over a thousand women living in Wyoming, and with their votes added to around six thousand men's votes, the state might be able to join the Union.

This surprising happening sent Susan Anthony into a storming rage. The Eastern suffragists had rallied for years and had resolved at their convention *"that it is the duty of the women of this country to secure for themselves the sacred right to the elective franchise."* But Wyoming's women had given action to those words.

Mary and many of her friends felt that Anthony was reacting from jealousy over their success.

Chapter 30

A New Beginning

Every day, Mary found her days turning into a dull routine; mundane, tiresome. Lectures were attended by many of the same women, suffragists, and ladies who were looking for something to do with their spare time. She knew that after attending a lecture, they would go home and soon forget most of what they had heard.

Without knowing the exact reason, Mary felt it was suddenly necessary to get on with writing and publishing the book she had thought about so many times. She had already written articles of the same nature for women's magazines. So, it seemed logical to start there, reciting many of those sentiments again.

That's what she would do. Go home to Oswego and write a book, maybe two. The first result she entitled *"Hit."*

When Mary began writing the book, she started with the thoughts closest to her heart: love and marriage. These two occurrences had brought forth many emotions that had been welling up in her thoughts for years, well suppressed and waiting to come bursting out. She was now thirty-nine years old.

The first chapter she entitled "Love and Marriage." Perhaps that was what she felt the strongest about at the time. She wrote enthusiastically, covering the topic from many angles.

"*There can be a beautiful confidence where soul reads soul,*" she wrote, no doubt reflecting back in memory on how she had felt when they (she and Albert) were "*akin in the same skin.*" She concluded that such a love was rare.

Another sentiment that she often recited was: "How barbarous the very idea of one equal promising to be the slave of another, instead of both entering life's greatest drama as intelligent equal partners. Our promises were such as denoted by two intelligent beings instead of one intelligence and one chained."

Sometimes in long rambling sentences she philosophized that if a woman had really been free to select a husband and was not pushed by well-meaning friends and family, she would not have married him. She speculated that parents were often to blame in looking for security for their daughters. She urged a bride to take a second look at the man she was considering. Was she looking through romanticized glasses?

Mary probably couldn't reflect upon her own marriage without recalling how eager her own friends and family had been to bring she and Albert together. She recognized her own parents' dedication to each other as a close example. For her visit to England, Mary had read about Queen Victoria's devotion and marriage to Prince Albert and the confrontations they had overcome. She wrote: "*There should be a perfect freedom for women to select a partner for life in a straight forward, honest and honorable manner.*"

For several months, Mary concentrated on her writing. It resulted in an eight-chapter book of essays expressing her strongest views on love, marriage and divorce, temperance, tobacco, labor, religion, and dress reform. Throughout the book ran a thread-like theme connecting "love and marriage" to every chapter, including temperance and smoking. In one way or another, she kept letting those emotions effect the success of a marriage.

One of her strongest comments which she no doubt repeated in numerous lectures, was the exclamation: How barbarous the very idea of one equal promising to be the slave of another, instead of both entering life's greatest drama as intelligent equal parties. Our promises were such as denoted by two intelligent beings instead of one intelligence and one slave.Upon its completion, Mary hoped her words would "hit the mark" with her readers. She dedicated the book to her parents, as well as practical dress reformers and professional sisters. The intent of the book was to *"emancipate you [women] from the bondage of all that is oppressive."*

She could now sell this small volume for a few pennies at her lectures or give it away. Once she completed the book, she felt inspired to continue. What more could she say? She kept writing as she continued to travel from Oswego to her lectures in Washington and elsewhere.

Regained enthusiasm

During the same period, she felt energized again by finding the time to help Frederick Douglas organize a rally. Douglas had established himself as a prominent abolitionist known throughout the United States and Europe. He and his wife had become strong advocates of the Black Women's suffrage campaigns, organized and active in the southern states. Now, he had come again to lead another rally in Washington. It seemed appropriate to join with him.

While in a writing routine, Mary continued to outline a second book. In it, she wanted to more directly express her candid opinions about men and how she felt they should act as human beings. This was a book she felt compelled to write because there were few of its kind available outside the medical field. She also knew that most women would find the topics repulsive but possibly enlightening. It dealt with the morals of men.

Probably because she knew she would receive severe criticism, possibly even threats, Mary did not use her name as the author. *"Unmasked, or The science of immorality"* stated it was written, "By A Woman Physician and Surgeon: to gentlemen."

In her rambling sentence style, Mary wrote twelve chapters condemning men for their aggression, abuse, intimidation, deceitfulness, and degradation of women. She led off with a rousing introduction, then proceeded to question "pure manhood."

Chapters on kissing, morning sickness in men, bareness, hymens, hernia, and hermaphrodites followed and included bodily sketches. The longest chapter was Chapter X on Social Evils, making up nearly half the book. A healthy review of Reform Dress was included, supported by over two dozen testimonials from noteworthy social and medical persons.

This book expressed another side of Mary Walker. She did not promote the book, but appeared to give copies away to medical and temperance friends. She did denote something of a changed viewpoint: *"Nothing less than perfect equality of rights will ever result in the greatest happiness, and the greatest possibilities."*

Mary was now forty-six years old.

Time marches on

As weary as it all sometimes seemed, Mary was still intent on keeping her hand in politics. It was a time when everyone seemed to have a cause to promote.

While Mary had been writing, Rutherford B. Hayes had been elected the 19th President (1877 to 1881). Although Hayes was a Republican, he had many attributes that Mary could appreciate.

During the war, he had served in the Shenandoah Valley. He had been admired by his soldiers and rose in rank to a brigadier. He had returned home to Ohio to serve as a congressman and later as Ohio's governor. He appeared to be ideally prepared to bring the Reconstruction period to a conclusion and welcome a feeling of modernization to the country. His reputation was unblemished; he was honest, steadfast, and moral. He and his wife, Lucy, strongly advocated for temperance.

On April 15, 1878, Mary began fighting a severe case of pneumonia. For several weeks thereafter she remained back on the farm recovering and planning. Six months later she had regained her health and spirit and was once again anxious to hit the lecture trail, traveling this time into New England and New York. She still felt strongly that her efforts there could carry some influence. She still felt that she was of value to herself and to the cause.

Day by day, reporting of the suffragist's activities had faded to the back pages of the newspapers, if they were mentioned at all. Westward interest continued. The railroads were carrying more people into the Midwest and then beyond. Problems with the Indians threw attention on the droves of westbound settlers and railroad builders.

During this time, Mary suffered a personal sorrow. Her

father, Avah Walker, passed away, leaving her the family farm and a one-thousand-dollar mortgage against it. At the time, her mother was eighty years old and in failing health. As her sisters had married very well, Mary's father must have thought he was helping her with security for her future. But in fact, she knew, that the small amount of income she could make from local doctoring would not support herself, her mother, and the farm. She would have to look elsewhere.

Back on the national scene, James A. Garfield had been elected President, but was assassinated after holding office from March to September. Once again, Mary grew sad and depressed, remembering how she had felt when President Lincoln had been killed.

In the country, particularly in Washington, something new was needed. She wondered whether the Vice President, Chester A. Arthur, could not only fill the presidential vacancy, but the need

A renewed effort

Up to this point, Mary's past requests for an increase in her wartime pension had been ignored. She had been making inquiries on this topic since 1871—for about five years now. Badgering was a better term for it. She had tried sending personal testimonies, affidavits, and other documentation, even for a time asking for a settlement due to her health and eye deterioration since leaving Castle Thunder. Her pension of eight dollars and fifty cents didn't go very far.

No matter how much she tried to save, there was never enough. She walked everywhere around Washington, giving up riding the trolley or city transporter. She ate very little, which she realized affected her health as well. Then finally, in

1890, her pension was adjusted to twenty dollars a month. Not satisfying, but eleven dollars and fifty cents more. That was the end of that.

Even in Washington, resorting back to a steady medical practice was out as well. After all these years, female doctors still were not being readily accepted. Searching out some type of federal job around the Capitol seemed to be her best alternative.

Once again, Mary resumed her letter writing campaign, sending her resume to every politician on her list and making inquiries as she circulated around the Capitol. In fact, she even included President Garfield, members of his Cabinet, as well as staffers on her appeals list. She now suggested to all of them that she was experienced as a letter writer, as well as writing for newspapers and magazines. She was seeking a clerk or secretary's position.

Mary prayed that local politicians who had successfully found positions would remember that she had supported them. It seemed to her that many political favors were being paid off with jobs in the various government departments.

Persistence pays off

Mary was persistent. She persevered. Her efforts finally paid off. She was offered a mail clerk's position in the Pension Office of the Department of the Interior and reported for work in April 1882. Yes, she did feel disappointed and degraded because the job offered none of the amenities she had received in other positions as a suffragist, such as days off or occasional meals. But she felt that her circumstances had become desperate. In November, just six months away, she would be fifty years old.

During the times when Mary had lived back at the farm,

she had planted a garden, and dried and canned vegetables. She had welcomed others to contribute to sharing the comforts of her home. Most of those efforts had not worked out well. At least now, with a federal position, she would be earning a regular income.

Mary had never before worked at a regular, daily job. Her type of discipline had always been self-imposed by whatever necessity arose. Also, many of her new co-workers immediately irritated her. Vice versa, she annoyed them. Many did not share her viewpoint on the right to vote, nor the reform dress issue. As a part of her dress, she also persisted in wearing "that Medal" even though the war was long over.

By now Mary had experimented with many combinations of dress, including her favorite pants with vest and frock coat. Her co-workers were shocked. Women simply did not wear pants! If they did, certainly not prancing around in public.

Mary was also accustomed to freely voicing her opinion. But it was plain that her co-workers were not prepared to accept her frequent absences. For in fact, Mary was still continuing to give lectures around Washington and to march in rallies whenever one was scheduled. She would also give herself a day off, without seeking permission, to tend to other activities she put on her calendar, such as attending other suffragists' lectures or visiting politicians' offices. To most of her co-workers, she was too much of a free spirit!

However, while on the job a new interest did intrigue her: the mailing of letters to special people such as the President of the United States, a Senator, or a General. In addition to regular mail, she had many times sent "special delivery" letters. She had often wondered whether those letters had been received by the addressee. In fact, she took it upon herself to start investigating this type of delivery service. Without consulting anyone, she began going around the city to various postal offices and inquiring how their mailings were handled. She discovered something interesting.

Although there were some inconsistencies, one common form of special delivery was to attach to the letter an envelope that would be returned to the sender upon its arrival at the correct destination. Mary proposed that doing away with the envelope would be more efficient. In fact, she even talked with the Postmaster General, who was surprisingly receptive to her idea.

One discovery was that around three million letters and packages were circulated back through the postal system because the addressees could not be found. Most landed in what was called the "dead letter office."

Letters and even packages were frequently addressed just to a person and a city. No other information, such as a street or building designation, was included. A frequent example was that the address would simply be to a first name and surname in Washington City. Perhaps there might be as many as fifteen or more persons by that name living in Washington or somewhere in the surrounding area.

As Mary gathered this information, she also began making the rounds of the Congressional offices inquiring about their letter handling experiences. This particular mailing problem was a topic that she found Congressmen were willing to talk with her about.

Finally, Mary proposed at a postal committee meeting a new idea for handling "special mailings." It was simple: do away with the envelope and simply attach a return postcard to the letter. When the letter reached the right person, the receipt would be signed with the correct name and address and returned to the sender. This procedure was to be called a "registered letter." The postal service was agreeable to testing this new method across the country.

Mary was ecstatic!

To her it brought personal satisfaction just to hear the admiration in the voices of the Congressmen who later came around to compliment her on her idea. It was working out and was proposed to be continued as a new policy in the United States Postal System. Hurrah, Mary concluded. For her, it was a small victory.

Despite the adoption of her new letter idea, Mary continued to be criticized heavily by her co-workers. Absenteeism on a regular basis was their major complaint. The newspapers caught wind of this rumor and expanded on the topic that the Medal of Honor recipient did not do her share of the work and that upon occasion, Mary had displayed a violent temper toward her co-workers. Subsequently, Mary was fired!

In response, she filed a rebuttal claim in her own defense.

Upon reviewing Mary's claim and hearing witnesses' testimony, the attorney general's ruling stood. Even though Mary recognized that much of the information presented was true, it was still a bitter situation. She had begun working at the postal position in April 1881 and was fired in June 1882. So, after about a year she was back in a desperate positionwith no income. She had to consider it a year lost!

Chapter 31

A Night to Remember

For Mary, there was one memorable, exciting, and splashing night during that year of 1882. It was an official invitation to attend a reception at the Whiter House.

Mary must have read and re-read the invitation many times. She was thrilled beyond words, yet hesitant. It was a formal piece of paper, of the finest quality, and bearing the distinguished crest of the President of the United States, Chester A. Arthur. She had not been this excited for a long, long time. Besides being impressed that someone there would even remember her, Mary was also bursting with curiosity. Mr. Arthur had already caused quite a stir in recent weeks with his refurbishing of the White House. Now, Mary was going to get to see it.

There had already been many newspaper accounts written about the newly redecorated White House. Mary even thought it amusing to read how the President personally had loaded up some twenty wagonloads of broken dishes and glassware, toys and trash from basement to attic and sent it off to be disposed of in some way. It had been collected and accumulated over the past twenty years, the newspapers reported.

As usual, Mary gave a great deal of thought to what she

should wear. She finally decided to keep it plain with the Medal of Honor pinned on her simple frock jacket over her dark pants and, her customary black bow tie. After all, this was the Arthur's big night

That evening, Mary waited impatiently for the White House carriage to arrive, watching the gray January clouds gather along the row of roof tops across the avenue. At last, she heard the sounds of wheels and hooves on the brick laid street. Already anxious to be on her way, Mary rushed out onto the porch and met the startled driver before he even had time to dismount from the driver's seat.

In the glow from the street lamps, the landau drawn by two matched horses loomed as splendidly as even Cinderella might have wished.

Listening to the horses' hooves all the way to the White House, Mary secretly reveled in the royal feeling of the ride. She really would have to make a journal entry of this night. However, as Mary often acknowledged, she was not one to readily writing in a journal.

Chester A. Arthur was a good six feet tall; Mary stood one foot less. Yet, as she took the President's hand warmly in greeting, she thought it a much further distance as she looked up into his face. Next to the President stood his sister, Mrs. Mary McElroy, who acted as the official White House hostess since her brother was a widower. Mary guessed it was probably Mrs. McElroy or one of her staff that was responsible for inviting her.

Although Mrs. McElroy was gowned exquisitely, Mary's attention was stolen instantly by the tall screen beside her. It was an elegant Tiffany glass screen with lights streaming through it in stained mosaic patterns. It lent splashes of light to the rows of palms lining the corridor directly behind it.

The magnificence of the sight had Mary spellbound. So much so, that she barely noticed the other guests wandering around. They seemed equally amazed. For the most part they were Congressmen and their wives, the men scowling at the expensive taste of the new interior and their wives overjoyed at the beautiful sights. There for all to view and inspect was the Blue Parlor, the Red Parlor, the Green Parlor.

Mary had heard and read frequentmentions of the official meeting rooms. But now, as she wandered along, tilting and craning her head to see the newly ornamented plaster ceilings, she felt as though she had known them always, for they held warmth and friendliness and even individualistic personalities.

Mary thought the Blue Room was indeed a most serene and peaceful "robin egg hue." Sobriety fell on her like a cloak as she moved on into the Red Parlor. Here the ceiling was of gold, glinting and twinkling with copper and bronze star insets. A stalwart air of patriotism flicked from the gas chandeliers onto the eagle and flag frieze motifs and magnificently carved wooden mantel.

But even more spectacular, Mary may have thought, was the Green Room. When she entered it, she was glad she had saved its inspection until last.

All the furnishings there were upholstered in a fine satin of the palest Nile green. The walls had been stained with a gilt substance, and on either side of the fireplace stood two Chinese vases, measuring at least four feet in height.

Convinced thoroughly of the Arthurs' good taste, Mary by-passed the remaining rooms open for inspection and drifted toward the Conservatory. Few other guests were there, yet it was, Mary felt, every bit as impressive as any of the upstairs parlors.

Grottoes and rookeries had been built into natural arrangements. To enhance the setting, ferns and tropical palms had been planted so as to grow in arches above the pathways. A second flight of stairs descended to a lower room where camellias and orchids were blooming.

Retracing her steps back up the staircase. Mary sauntered along the hall. Quite unexpectedly, she came upon the Oriental delegation leaning against the wall. Their faces were like expressionless masks. Their wooden-straight figures billowed with padded bouffant coats and full trousers. For a moment, Mary thought they were artificial.

"Amelia Bloomer," she said between her teeth.

"Good evening," came a reply.

Startled Mary turned, then flushed in embarrassment as she feared her comment might have been overheard. She realized, too, that the man was making a great effort to be polite, for he was also dressed identically to all of the others.

"I am Dr. Mary Edwards Walker," Mary smiled warmly and bowed slightly, feeling some of her composure returning. She extended her hand,

"Ah yes," the man replied. Immediately, Mary noted the slender length of his fingers and the paleness of his skin as he extended his hand toward her.

"I am the War Minister of China, Ting Fang," he spoke clearly.

Mary held her breath waiting for the next comment from him, but it did not come.

"I noticed that President Arthur has used many lovely oriental objects in his redecorating," Mary remarked. "Especially those two large vases by the hearth in the Green Parlor. Lovely,

lovely," she almost whispered.

"We are deeply honored that he has chosen to include them."

The war minister bowed politely, but made no further motion to move away. This time Mary remained silent, until at last, the war minister cleared his throat. It was obvious a question was forming.

"Gracious doctor," he began, "Pardon my insatiable curiosity, for it is sometimes my nature. But why do you wear these?" He pointed to Mary's trousers.

"Why?" Mary thought on that question a moment. She had to think of an answer that would be an illustration, just as though she was explaining something to a child. Then a reasonable reply came to her.

She smiled at the Minister, "I wear these trousers for the same reason that you are wearing a gown."

"Ah," he grinned, "because it is the custom of my country."

Mary shrugged in a most Yankee-like manner. "America is a free country isn't it, Mr. Fang? As long as it remains so, I may wear whatever I please. A gown like yours or trousers like these."

"That is true," agreed the War Minister of China, ending with a chuckle.

"It has been my humblest pleasure to meet a woman of your ...." he faltered, seeking to translate his Chinese to its proper meaning in English. "I have heard the use of the word 'metal' to describe a person of your deeds."

Mary nodded trying to decipher what he meant. Before she could reply, he went on.

"To my mind, however, comes a more appropriate material, one of strength of character. You, Dr. Walker, are something like the jade. A substance of durability and dependence. Yet, there is a beauty too."

Mr. Fang moved away followed by his delegation, while Mary stood hypnotically under his spell. Unconsciously, her hand moved to touch her hair, then her cheek. Thoughtfully, her hand strayed to touch the medal, as though to confirm that it was still there.

It hardly mattered at all that the room was rapidly filling with ladies gowned in rich velvets and silks, wide skirts sweeping the floor. Or that the dining tables blossomed with gilt candlesticks and the daintily chosen Garfield china of pinky-beige. Even the food could have been the fried mush of the Ohio regiment and Mary would not have noticed.

Although the clock had not struck twelve yet, Mary Walker was ready to go home. This evening had truly given her a Cinderella dream to cherish. What could be next for a fifty-year-old woman, she wondered.

Not surprisingly, her presence at the White House tour was mentioned in the newspapers. Dr. Mary Edwards Walker was still considered to be "good copy." From the journalists' viewpoint, she was a "likeable character about Washington." She seemed to frequently be on the fringe of being in the spotlight, reporters and residents often pointing her out to the city's visitors. She often became a story herself without intending to be.

Who knew when or where Dr. Mary Walker might show up? And a reporter would write a line or two about her for one of the local newspapers.

A friendship lost

During this same time period, Mary's long time dear friend,

Belva Lockwood, announced her candidacy for President of the United States. She was representing the National Equal Rights Party. Her opponent was Grover Cleveland. She had begun her campaign earlier in1884 and admitted that she probably could not win. Then some confusion arose about her running mate for Vice President. Strong sentiment was for Fredrick Douglas. But that announcement later proved to be misinformation.

Because of their long friendship, Belva may have assumed or hoped that Mary would offer her experience in setting up rallies or campaign on her behalf. Sadly, Mary declined supporting her, and their friendship began to cool.

There were probably many reasons for Mary's decision. For one, Grover Cleveland offered stronger executive experience for the presidency. He had begun his career as a sheriff, mayor of Buffalo, New York, and Governor of the state. His platform had always been as a political reformer, particularly against favoritism.

Belva did offer several good ideas. She agreed with Cleveland that political reform was needed. She set up a twelve-point platform that included foreign affairs, women's rights, and civil service reforms.

There was no doubt that Mary admired Belva for her principles and perseverance through the years. From time to time, the two women may have mentored one another. Because of their interest in civil law, they had probably discussed many cases. But Belva had no executive experience. In earlier years, she had successfully lobbied Congress to permit women lawyers to practice before the Supreme Court. Unfortunately, with her bid for the presidency, Belva irritated several suffragists who spoke out against her. calling her arrogant and pretentious. Although those women could not vote, they could become influential in opposing her platform. Sadly, she was nicknamed "Old Lady Lockwood" by the *Atlanta Constitution*.

In November, Belva Lockwood, who had been recognized as the first woman presidential candidate, surprisingly did receive over four thousand votes from men.

This had been a difficult decision for Mary to keep. It cost her a personal friend. There could be no recovery, as Belva

Lockwood stubbornly continued her quest, campaigning up until 1888 against Benjamin Harrison.

Nothing was happening

Once again, weeks and months blended into years as Mary Walker wrote, lectured, performed domestic chores, and in general, persevered. By train, she moved between her Oswego farm home and events in Washington, and around to other cities where suffragists gathered. Many tasks became repetitious.

And then it happened. An exciting new adventure entered Mary's life.

Chapter 32

An Exciting Change

"One Dime! It only costs one Dime!" A barker stood outside the Cincinnati Vine Street Museum & Palace Theater in Cincinnati, Ohio and shouted at the top of his voice.

"Stay the day! See the world's most exciting treasures! Stay as long as you like!"

It was called a Dime Museum. While barkers shouted outside, curious people spent a dime to enter America's newest attraction. It was a new form of entertainment that combined snatches of stage shows, carnival highlights, education, and all types of enlightenment from around the world.

A few years earlier, P.T. Barnham had set up a similar house of entertainment in New York City called the American Museum. He then went on to place a greater emphasis on his circus enterprises. But other promoters invested in the idea and reinvented it.

It was 1887, a year that promised to be an interesting one for Mary Walker. But nothing could be more promising than the opportunity to work for the Dime Museum organization. By now she was not afraid of adventure, nor trying something new. She was fifty-five years old, and this was a challenge that she readily accepted.

For once, Mary Walker was in the right place at the right time.

More than a sideshow

It was called The Chicago Museum, but was also known as the Kohl and Middleton Vine Street Dime Museum. It had opened its doors under the auspices of the Kohl and Middleton Agency, a reputable theatrical company. It was a stable enterprise that produced a variety of entertainment and stage programs across the country. It was more than a sideshow, although some people called it that. It had expanded its business to build similar museums in Toledo, Cincinnati, Buffalo, Detroit, and New York City.

Now as an employee of Kohl and Middleton, Mary became part of the entertainment team that traveled the circuit of the different museums. Another group formed by the same association was called the Wonderland Museums. Often, the entertainers and speakers would interchange.

Cincinnati's thriving Vine Street Dime Museum & Palace Theater was one of their best examples. It was housed in a multiple storied building, constructed inside with several small stages, lecture rooms, and a larger theater where hourly stage productions were presented. The museum was designed to offer both live entertainment, as well as giving visitors an opportunity to browse the tangible Wonders of the World. Display cases lined the rooms. Other exotic items hung from the walls in permanent showings. "Educational" was how they described the tapestries, artwork, and taxidermy objects.

The Vine Street Dime Museum also prided itself on its collection of sideshows revolving around tattooed men, bearded women, Siamese twins, midgets, albino persons, and other human deformities. In addition, there were skilled performers such as knife throwers, sharp shooters, and exotic animals from around the world. Stage presentations ranged from Shakespearian plays to minstrel shows. Add to that several scientific experts, including Mary Walker, who offered lectures on her favorite topics of women's hygiene, temperance, marriage, and women's rights.

To Mary, this became a weird and wonderful world. It was one that she must have come to enjoy being a part of because she continued her association with it for nearly four years. After spending some years back in Oswego, she came back to rejoin them again in 1893.

It was a strange environment and certainly a departure from her previous forms of livelihood as a physician, soldier, suffragist, and postal worker. She still considered herself to be in good health. And, she had found a reason to be upbeat again.

But most appealing was the fact that the Museum paid her "one hundred fifty dollars" a month. That solved some of Mary's most pressing financial problems, including taxes that were due on the farm in Oswego.

Mary had immediately recognized this as a terrific opportunity that suited both her personality and her purpose. She had already adjusted to being called a "freak" and a "crazy lady." Now, she seemed right at home amid abnormal creatures, tattooed men and women, living skeletons, exotic birds, snakes, and reptiles.

They became her traveling companions, acquaintances, sometimes a patient and in a way, an extended family. In addition to having her own lecture stage, she was joined by productions such as *Uncle Tom's Cabin* or actors reciting from

Shakespeare. On some days, she found herself lecturing while next door in another lecture room an accomplished carver might be whittling down a chunk of wood.

While traveling and speaking, Mary continued selling her books and enjoyed a way of life that many an observer might have called a Bohemian lifestyle. She dished out her opinion about hygienic practices, about love and marriage, fidelity and morality, women's rights and religion, and condemned alcohol consumption and smoking. Most of her comments were taken directly from her own book, *Hit*. It served as her handbook and she felt repeating its contents brightened the days of the women who heard her. She hoped some of them practiced her advice!

Upon occasion, she was prepared to practice medicine among her fellow companions. She sassed police and achieved a line or two now and then in the local newspapers. She still made good copy.

While lecturing at the Wonderland Museum in Toledo in March, a member of her audience was a young reporter with the *Toledo Blade* who later observed in his newspaper that "she had fallen from the platform of Princes to the stage of Freaks."

"Words will never hurt me," she had responded, or words to that effect, when newspapers criticized her for associating herself with such "freak" shows.

Another world's fair

During this span of years, considerable excitement was also being created by fairs and expositions that were being held around the world. They were favored by the public for their entertainment and educational contributions. In America, these events brought out large gatherings of suffragists, parading in all white dresses as they continued to stress their cause.

One of the most exciting happenings of the time came in 1893, when Mary was traveling the second time with the Museum group. It was the World's Fair Exposition in Chicago. For two years representatives from New York City and Chicago had battled as to which city would be awarded the Fair. In the end, that "upstart city in the prairie" won out.

Of course, as daring as Mary had become, she must have put that event on her calendar. It would have been only a train ride away.

The Fair became a great time for suffragists from around the world to gather and march, give speeches, and taunt the public. In actuality, it was a celebration of the Four Hundred Anniversary of Columbus discovering America. It was laid out on the shore of Lake Michigan and lasted for several months.

This was the site of George Ferris' "wonder of the world" invention called the Ferris Wheel. Thirty-six glass boxes were built to hold together on a giant metal wheel. Up to forty people could be seated inside each box on wire chairs that were then lifted forty feet above the ground.

When the Fair ended, it seemed the country went back to normal.

Recognized

Mary continued to be frequently recognized as the "lady who wore pants," even though wearing pants was no longer a "hot topic." More women were beginning to wear pants or overalls, but they were not attracting the same amount of publicity that Mary had in the past and continued to attract now. Most were not as outspoken either. Now, she could dress as outlandish as she pleased.

But she still held one distinction that she proudly touted. She was the only woman to have received the Medal of Honor. She treasured it. She wore it daily. She still lectured outside the museum when the opportunity arose. Women who attended her lectures were still in awe of her adventures.

Yes, she admitted upon occasion, she was making a spectacle of herself. And yes, she knew that many times she ruffled the feathers of both her friends in Washington and her family back home in Oswego. Her sisters and their families often could not escape being embarrassed by her antics. And for this she may have been sorry. But she persevered. As many reassured her, *"her cause was just."* The rights of women were still held in bondage.

Keeping busy

In 1901, Mary had joined Kansas temperance leader Carrie Nation in condemning the administration of William McKinley. Over a ten-year period, Caroline "Carrie" Nation had gained a lot of newspaper space as a strong temperance advocate in Kansas. Her husband had died of alcoholism and in almost a revenge rampage, she had set out to destroy Kansas' saloons. She was strongly supported by the Women's Christian Temperance Association. Often accompanied by hymn-singing women, she would march into a bar, sing and pray while smashing bar stock and fixtures with a hatchet. Many of her values coincided with Mary's. She, too, condemned women wearing tight fitting garments, especially corsets. And she suspected, as Mary did, that President McKinley was a secret drinker.

Another strange thing happened. Sometime in 1907,

Mary received a second Medal of Honor. There was not very much notoriety about it. But, being curious as always, Mary made inquiries. It was unusual.

She learned that in 1902, the Army had changed the ribbon suspending the medal. "Something more should have been done to distinguish it. The Medal's design should have been changed," spoke out Brigadier General George Gillespie, a Civil War veteran and a Medal recipient.

Gillespie felt strongly about this change. He then took it upon himself to push for a redesign, going so far as to have Horace Porter, the Ambassador to France, have a French company create a new design. It was submitted for approval to Elihu Root, Secretary of War, the Army Board, and to Congress, and approved April 23, 1904. Both ribbon and medal were changed. It was then minted and distributed to past recipients that could be found.

Mary was noticed upon at least one occasion wearing the second medal beside the first. But her sentiments stayed with her preference for the original award.

During that time, Mary also felt a short-lived inspiration to enter the political arena herself. She announced that she would campaign for a seat in the United States Senate. Her platform would be against the use of tobacco and alcohol.

Almost immediately upon making her announcement, friends convinced her that such a platform would never be supported. She withdrew in frustration.

Chapter 33

The Way Grows Weary

It was a time filled with sad news. Many of the women who, at one time or another, seemed to have been Mary's role models died. Elizabeth Blackwell died in England and her sister, Emily Blackwell, died three months later. Dorothea Dix also passed away.

Mary had known the Blackwell's and women who had crusaded in other states only by reputation. But she visualized their faces from photographs and sketches she had seen. All had been dedicated and determined women. She did not feel she could give up their fight just because they were gone. Their passing seemed to revive her strength and determination. She now felt more resolute than ever before.

Mary reflected that soon, she would be too old and unsteady to carry on. But in those remaining days she promised herself that she was going to demand the privileges due to an old, eccentric woman.

"Oh, let them say what they might." But from now on, however short a time, she would be a thorn in the side of Congress. She would do her part to make each day one step closer to the time when women would be granted equal rights.

But not all women were interested in, or eager for, the vote.

As suffragists' movements had grown in both the United States and Great Britain, so had opposing organizations. In 1911 an anti-suffragist group called The National Association to Oppose Women's Suffrage was formed in Mary's home state. Its membership was made up of both women and men. It had a strong appeal with New York State women and expanded to other Eastern states.

Hundreds of cartoons depicting deprived husbands and children appeared in Great Britain and America, particularly in Eastern cities. Fathers were shown at the washing board doing the laundry or hugging the children while Mom danced.

"Don't marry a suffragist!" urged one poster. That women were already "free in their homes" became a deep sentiment. One *New York Times* cartoon showed a woman hugging a rug. This new anti-movement was all just another thorn to contend with, argued suffragist leaders.

Mary flung herself deeper and more earnestly into her "constitutional" project. She had been studying these laws for several years now. Relentlessly, she stalked the corridors of the Senate and House where she button-holed Congressmen and plagued them for hours. She was not to be put off lightly this time!

Mary began preparing the outline for her Constitutional talk. Writing by hand could become an arduous project in itself. She fondly entitled her assault the *"Crowning Constitutional Argument."* When completed, her arguments would have to be first presented to the Congressional House Committee working on the subject.

Fortunately, Mary was already acquainted with most of the men appointed to this particular committee, and their presence bolstered her strength. She certainly did not want any of them to feel pity for this old woman. Instead, she chose to meet them on their own battleground in a committee meeting room. She had it scheduled.

Committee meetings were more intimate than speaking to the full Congress. They were generally held in a small side room, with the congressmen and speaker seated at a table surrounded by an audience seated in chairs.

"Any law of the State," Mary pointed out vigorously in the course of her arguments, *"which denies women any privileges enjoyed by men are hereby declared to be in conflict with the Constitution of the United States."*

Mary recited other passages of law, gave examples; even directed their attention to a woman's position in countries like England. Yes, the day will come, she promised them and herself when women would rightfully be recognized.

"Magnificent, Dr. Walker." One member of the Committee came forward to speak with her. He was a man much her same age, white hair, his voice soft and gentle in the tones of the South. Strangely, she felt as though she had seen this man somewhere before, but his image was not clear in her memory. He went on talking.

"I remember hearing a similar address you gave some years back on this subject. I believe at that time Chief Justice Salmon Chase presided over the gathering. I know it is difficult, but you must be patient."

Instantly, Mary recalled her meeting with the Chief Justice. Senator Charles Sumner had been among those in her presence. Mary wondered if this was …? His eyes were clear and steady. Slowly he reached out and took May's hand. She wondered whether he saw the faint blue veins trailing up into her slender wrist.

"You, Dr. Walker, have helped open the door through

which all women will yet walk to vote."

Mary smiled humbly. She had been about to retort, but instantly realized it was not the appropriate time. Over the years, she had taught herself to keep her mouth shut—bite her tongue, so to speak. She was getting used to being placated. But he had seemed sincere.

Everyone here in this magnificent building was sincere, but nothing was happening. The Committee chair promised to consider her speech further. But she also recognized that Congressional folks had a tendency to talk a lot about things but end up with no action.

So, Mary continued to haunt the Congressional corridors for many days afterward. She had her Constitutional paper printed into a pamphlet that she handed out on every occasion. She wanted to make her frock coat and striped trousers a familiar sight to everyone. She wanted to keep reminding them of her purpose.

A new era begins

Sadly, Mary realized that no one wanted to listen to a wacky old woman's ramblings about a tired subject. Yes, that was what they called her and worse. She represented the past, the hard times, the Civil War. Politicians and businessmen had no time to think of that now. It was the beginning of a new era.

In the months that passed, both political and economic tensions mounted across the Atlantic. Mary read avidly about the happenings in Europe The European nations hovered dangerously on the brink of war. Newspapers were crowded with headlines of nations squaring off against one another.

The topic of suffrage in America was pushed off even the back pages of the newspapers, as well as to the back of everyone's mind.

Still there were a few known women around the country and in Washington who carried on the fight. That year, at the biennial meeting of the General Federation of Women's Clubs, Mary was invited to participate. As she entered the old Seventh Regiment Armory where the meeting was being held, she suddenly felt inspired to say a few words of encouragement to this group of younger women. She was overwhelmingly surprised to find them both receptive and extremely interested in many of her comments about clothing.

"What kind of hose do you wear, Dr. Walker?" was one of the questions asked from the audience. "What kind of shoes?"

Mary obligingly showed them the kind of stockings that she wore. They were a plain durable type. She could tell at once that they were thinking of the newer styled half-hose.

"Since I am an old woman," she pointed out to them, "I feel chills now that I once thought delightful. Halfway-hose I do not find warm enough." She then pointed to her shoes.

"I also choose a sensible and stout piece of footgear. In this way, I believe women can completely avoid blisters, bunions, bruises, and other kinds of foot troubles. Wear sturdy shoes," she urged. She was a good example of a woman who had walked many miles in canvassing and rallying. "Wear sturdy shoes" was one of the first pieces of advice sheemphasized.

At the end of her address, the group began to clap, slowly at first, then more vigorously. Then, one by one, they began to rise to their feet. Mary felt her eyes beginning to brim with tears that she did not even try to stop. A standing ovation was the greatest tribute she could possibly receive from an audience. There were no words left in her to express her appreciation and real joy.

Chapter 34

Joy Short Lived

Joy was short lived for Mary. Word arrived from friends in Washington that a meeting of the Board of Medal Awards had been called. The major reason for their assembly was to re-examine all the awards that had been presented during and after the Civil War and commemorating other events as well. One reason for the review was that some military pensions were tied to certain awards.

In fact, when Mary had received the second Medal of Honor, she may have questioned its authenticity relative to her service. At the time, several veterans' organizations had handed out medals honoring specific battles or deeds. Perhaps that was why she had seldom worn the second Medal.

When Mary reached the Capitol, she found the convening Board to be in a state of mixed opinions on the subject. She listened carefully to the arguments of the Review Board members. Mary even agreed with the Secretary of War in the belief that some Medals of Honor had been indiscriminately handed out at the close of the war. Some of the reasons for receiving medals had even been discovered to have been falsified. Particularly under the scrutiny of the Board, was the loose manner of distribution of one medal in particular—the Medal of Honor.

Through the long winter days that the Board consumed in hearings and examinations, Mary waited patiently in a nearby hotel. At last, in mid-February a final decision came. Sentiment rode high, but in the end, Mary received a cold curt appraisal, and any objections were heard by a patient mannered clerk in the War Department office.

"The Medal of Honor is bestowed upon those who risked their lives above and beyond the call of duty," he pointed out quietly. "In your case, Dr. Walker, there were no questionable factors."

Mary waited for the clerk to continue. The room was deadly silent. Finally, he gave an explanation.

"One is the fact that the occasion for your presentation was not properly recorded in the War Department Archives."

The clerk cleared his throat and dared to glance up at Mary's face. "Secondly, the law reads that you must have been involved in actual conflict with an enemy. Now, from what evidence we have here, you were awarded the Medal solely on your bravery and valuable service."

Mary did not know whether she could trust her voice to be steady or not as she asked: "This examination by the Board is final then?"

The clerk nodded. "The Board of Officers was called together by the Secretary of War. I am sorry, but your name will be permanently stricken from the Medal of Honor list."

Mary turned her head slightly from the view of the clerk. She felt a tear in the corner of her eye.

"May I keep these medals?" She showed him the two she previously had been given. One was the original. The other was the second, redesigned medal.

The clerk glanced at the medals in her hand and shrugged. Mary moved slowly away. She knew he was embarrassed and perhaps didn't really care.

How many years had passed? Three dozen? More? Fifty years had passed and as easily as plucking petals from a flower, a medal had been given and then taken away. With a twinge of remorse, Mary returned the medals to her pocket. Now all she had was a chunk—no, chunks of metal. Two worthless bronze medals and a monthly pension of eight dollars and fifty cents. No, she corrected herself, she was now receiving twenty dollars. That represented the sum total of her award—the highest one's country could offer.

She laughed softly to herself, oblivious to the people passing near her. It was as though a joke had been played on her.

Mary took out the medals again and turned them over in her palm. Two cold pieces of medal that had taken her on a journey around the world. She wished she did not feel a bitterness. She should not, she told herself. Still, there were some things she could not forget. The sickness, the diseases, the starving—those she remembered had been her worst enemies.

Mary's fingers tightened around the medal disks as though she wished to squeeze the very coldness from them. But the saddest thing, she realized, was that after today her work in Washington was nearing an end.

Perhaps I am too old anyway, she told herself consolingly. She had already slipped one morning this month on the Capitol steps. The fall had hurt her leg, and possibly a fracture, although it was an impressive place to fall to her knees.

Mary must have knelt there before that noble mass of white columns and felt completely conquered and tired. At the time she was staying at the Lochraven Hotel in Washington.

She went there for a few days to nurse her leg and bruised knees and perhaps her pride. Afterward she had felt as though some of her confidence had drained away. She decided now to steady herself better by using a cane.

However, before leaving Washington, there was one other place she wanted to visit. And that was the newly completed headquarters of the American Red Cross.

It was a stately marble building and Mary agreed, a fitting monument to that girl, Clara Barton, who like herself had nursed the wounded under fire. Antietam, Vicksburg, Chancellorsville, and all those other places where women had administered to the wounded. This building had been dedicated to their memory.

"To those Heroic Women of the Civil War," read the inscription. Inside, a second similar tablet had also been placed. Silently Mary read its dedication:

"To the women of both the North and South, that their labors to the suffering and wounded might be perpetuated."

In hearing the words echo through her mind, Mary suddenly felt strengthened in the knowledge that she too could say that she was a part of this building. She was a part of the struggle that had been started by women on many battlegrounds. And, though that war had long been ended; another war was still with them as women fought to be free.

Retreat to Bunker Hill

The first sounds Mary must have heard when she awoke in the mornings at Bunker Hill Farm were the birds chirping and flitting among the trees. Although there were trees and birds available all over Washington , the country offered a quieter atmosphere than the noises often rising from the streets of the

Capitol. But even now that she was settling in at home, there were still disquieting times. Friends and family welcomed her, but some of her neighbors were disturbed by her return. Again, family members living nearby often found themselves embarrassed when she suddenly voiced her opinions too vocally.

Through the years, Mary had become involved in squabbles and a law suit or two with her neighbors and the townspeople, but now other problems began to arise. She had permitted some of her neighbors' cattle to feed on her grass. Some acreage had been farmed. She wanted that to stop. She wanted to be paid for its usage.

Mary had also continued sharing her home with friends or acquaintances, whether she was at home or not. Now, some people came to stay with her for days it seemed, sometimes pitching in and sharing with the farm's chores of gardening, canning, and harvesting; sometimes not. Those were the times when the townspeople were most weary that those strangers might become troublesome. After all, the town had grown larger and busier too.

Mary continued her practice of frequently writing letters to various newspapers around the country expressing her opinion on topics from Washington politics to global reflections. One topic she apparently took an interest in was strikes in American coal mines. The strikes had caused a shortage of coalminers.

Somewhere she must have learned that convicts were being used for labor in some mines. That sparked her opinion and a letter went out. She expressed her thought that reduced sentences should be given to such convicts. It made good copy. At least one editor must have thought so, for suddenly her sentiments turned up in print. Such appearances in a newspaper often drew reporters to seek her out to do follow-up articles.

These types of spontaneous responses also caused Oswego's townspeople to view Mary not so much as a disgruntled celebrity, but someone of curiosity that too often created the news.

These disruptions to her life caused Mary's temper to flare even more often. She would appear at the city's meetings to protest and argue. When strange faces appeared near her farm, neighbors complained that they were fearful, particularly at night. Members of Mary's family were also concerned that someone might take advantage of her hospitality. They argued and disagreed with her. To some extent, they were also being continually embarrassed by the publicity she received.

In addition, money was still scarce to meet her living expenses. Too often, live-in visitors would not contribute toward their stay, but Mary permitted them to stay on anyway. Even when she had lived in Washington City, she had enjoyed opening her home to others. She now also began to visit more with her neighbors upon whom she had come to depend on during the years. A few had become good friends.

But there was still one idea that Mary kept thinking about: "communal living." In fact, she had formed a strong favorable opinion about it. It was a social structure that had worked successfully with some religious colonies that had come to America. During her childhood, her father had welcomed visitors who had shared the Walker's home and become part of an extended family. Often, when she had shared her various homes in Washington, she had found it a comfortable way to live. It was also a reasonable way to survive.

Mary had thought often, even daydreamed from time to time, about the possibility of building a communal community. Now she had the opportunity to put her plan into action.

Her thirty-some unused acreage was an ideal place to start. For hours, Mary must have visualized how she might transform a part of the farm into such a communal colony.

She even considered what she might call it. The name "Adamless Colony" would express that it was an all-women's community where she might set up a training school for young women to learn nursing or caregiving, that would teach young women to practice nursing and caregiving. She strongly believed that every woman should have the opportunity to be self-supportive. She went so far as to outline her idea in an interview with a reporter for the popular *Metropolitan Magazine*.

This was news! It also greatly disturbed the citizens of Oswego.

Mary continued visualizing how it might function. Months later, when she had finalized her plan, she went before Oswego's city planners to further explain her idea. The citizens were outraged.

Absolutely not!

Immediately they overruled giving her permission! Again, it was not that the idea was impossible or impractical, but now they were further afraid of what problems the creation of such a female colony could produce.

For Mary, life on the farm was an adjustment. Many times, it was too quiet. As the day would end, she must have felt burdened with anxieties, not all financial. It was annoying to see weeds growing in the garden and not be able to put on her straw hat and spend the day pulling them. She had always relied on her ability to walk, to be mobile on almost any kind of terrain. Now she had become dependent on using a cane and had to be careful with every step.

Throughout the years, Mary had climbed hundreds of stairs leading in and out of the Capitol City's buildings and walked the gravel roads around them. It was different on the farm where tough grass and weeds grabbed and pulled at her cane. Keeping her balance was not easy. There were many activities around a farm that could throw a person off balance.

To add to her worries, she had also gained another mouth to feed. When her elder sister, Aurora, passed away she gave her horse and buggy to Mary in her will. A horse required more than just grass to eat. But she must have enjoyed getting out in the buggy and driving to town. There she would persuade or pay a nickel to some child to help her drop a metal stop at the horse's feet to keep it from walking away while she shopped.

It was told that one local boy had described to his school mates how his father had met her one day on the street and had given her a donation. She had thanked him with a tip of the hat she was wearing at the time.

Stories were always circulating around Oswego about Mary. She seemed to be a popular topic of conversation with the locals.

Once it was reported that a neighbor had seen her standing under an old tree on the farm bashing a wooden souvenir cane, given out during President William McKinley's election campaign, against the ground. It angered Mary that it had been McKinley who was responsible for directing the Army to set new policies for applicants applying for restoration of the Medal of Honor.

When she was confronted with the story, Mary admitted to having lost her temper. She remarked that she did not particularly like his policies. She had become angry and bashing his cane to splinters was how she was getting it out of her system.

Rumors such as that story easily sprang up and spread around the Oswego area. But generally, the most common remark about her was "that she wore pants," even though many women were now wearing "trousers," particularly those women working in factories. Across America, "pants" were becoming an everyday apparel.

Mail delivery was another frustration. It came too slowly. Mary had grown used to the Washington postal system while living there. Now it took forever, it seemed, for a reply to reach Bunker Hill Farm. Yet doggedly Mary kept sending her opinion off to people and newspapers she knew or responding to an editorial. After all, postage stamps only cost two cents.

For years, another of Mary's habits had been to pick up and read thrown-away newspapers. In Washington these periodicals could be found lying around public places, on tables, or dropped as trash by previous readers. Washington editions, mastheads from other states, international newspapers—all left along the way by lobbyists, Congressional staff, business men. This abundance of newspapers was no longer readily available.

Chapter 35

Twilight Journey

Mary Edwards Walker spent most of the remaining years of her life on her farm in Oswego, New York. As was her nature, she often fussed and sometimes feuded with her neighbors and the local government. There was still a sting to her remarks sometimes, and she stayed steadfast in giving her opinion. But she did have some friends and neighbors who were supportive.

Surprisingly, reporters still asked for interviews. Following an interview, one reporter with the *New York Times* wrote in its March 25, 1912 edition:

"She had a sort of dignity, and about her an essential goodness."

He had obviously found her mind still keenly alert. Yet the deep wrinkle pattern across her face was a testimony to her upcoming birthday. She would be ninety years old.

There were some luxuries to living on the farm. She could sleep late in the mornings if she chose. Taking naps and going to bed early were among the "hygienic" care giving recommendations emphasized by J.R. Trall at the Hygeia Therapeutic College.

Mary had concurred with Trall's teachings and not only probably included them in her own lectures, but put them into practice now and then. One of his primary teachings was about "convalescence," which Mary had prescribed whenever she could to a patient. He warned against making extra demands upon the energy and resources of a patient unless necessary. To maintain good health, he prescribed *"laying down in the day time, preferably after the noon meal, and having an hour or more of rest and, perhaps sleep. It is well to sleep at this time."*

Trall had also suggested such meditation practices as taking "time to watch green waves of verdure in one's surroundings. Observe the clumps of trees, the fields white with daisies, the lovely garden plots before rustic homes."

These caregiving health practices Mary could now practice herself.

Rumors of war

As the years advanced, Mary closely followed the growing controversies abroad on the Continent. Simultaneously, the news grew from the Western States. Sadly, very little advancement came on the home front for women's suffrage.

In 1914, Mary decided she wanted to join the Daughters of the American Revolution (DAR), headquartered in New York. She believed she qualified. They turned her down. She was told that her mode of dress was the real complaint against her being accepted. She became angry enough to fight them, except the St. Louis, Missouri, Chapter stepped in and was willing to give her a membership. She was content with that gesture.

On October 25, 1915, it was reported that Mary was among suffragist advocates who participated in a huge parade in New York City. Estimates as to the number of activists coming from around the world ranged as high as thirty thousand.

How these numbers were counted was questionable, but it seemed to attract a huge gathering and received extensive newspaper coverage.

In April 1917, the world heard once again from Mary Walker as a war became apparent in Europe. In patriotic sincerity, she sent a lengthy cable to Kaiser Wilhelm of Germany. She asked him to stop the war and invited him to meet in a peace conference with his American counterparts to be held at her Bunker Hill Farm. In her usual style she added a note that there could be no smoking nor drinking. Once again, she had made the news—or created it.

Casting a vote

Demonstrating at voting locations was another activity in which Mary could still participate. She had shown up several times during her lifetime at voting sites, requesting her right to vote. Of course, this annoyed poll officials, but it was all to no avail. Certainly, she did not hesitate to show up to cast a vote at her hometown elections, from which she was also turned away. Occasionally, it would get a line in a newspaper.

During this same period, Mary's health began to weaken. Even her fierce fighting spirit began fading. It was difficult to determine what may have been the cause. For persons of her age, a common cold could quickly become pneumonia and be difficult to diagnose.

Whatever the cause, for a short time it was reported that she became a patient at the General Army Hospital that had been built within Fort Ontario in 1917. By that time, the Fort had become a historic landmark, dating back to its original construction by the British Army in the 1700s on Lake Ontario and within the city of Oswego.

In Oswego, the Winter Solstice brought with it chilling winds across the lake and the ground became frozen. It became too cold to go out walking. Now and into February, Mary spent many of her days at the home of her long-time close friends and neighbor, the Dwyers. . There on February 21, 1919, she passed away.

Mary had requested that she be dressed in her customary black frock coat, vest, and tie. Quietly, she was buried in the Walker family plot nearby in Rural Cemetery. She was eighty-six years old.

One day later, on February 22, school children and businesses celebrated Washington's birthday—a national holiday.

Locally, her obituary appeared in her hometown paper. A few lines were printed in the *Washington Post* and *New York Times* on February 23, 1919.

"We live in deeds, not years," Mary Walker had written as the opening page of her book *Hit*, so many years earlier. It could have been her epitaph.

A year and a half later, in 1920, suffragists achieved their goal when the Nineteenth Amendment was added to the United States Constitution.

Chapter 36

A Word After

Decades passed. Now and then the name Mary Walker would appear in the newspaper, usually referenced in some women's history article. And as sometimes happens, a family member may recall a tidbit from its ancestry. Within the Walker family, their ancestor Mary was not completely forgotten.

In the late 1960s a grandniece, Helen Hays Wilson, began an inquiry into the restoration of her great aunt Mary Walker's Medal of Honor. She lived in Washington D.C., close to the location of several federal military review boards and record offices. She began lobbying Congressional members, their staffs, and other related departments and groups. Some interest was kindled particularly among women's organizations.

Each year Mrs. Wilson's campaign generated more interest, and she continued by by launching a more intensive and broader advocacy. She increased calling upon congressionally connected persons, as well as shifting stronger national pressure upon women's organizations. This was the beginning of a lengthy and arduous task

Thousands of letters and telephone calls went out. Newspapers were contacted across the country. In 1961 one newspaper contacted was *The Indianapolis Star*, where columnist Ben Cole subsequently interviewed Henry J. Baker, a Mary Walker kinsman..

Cole described how Baker had made an inquiry to Indiana Representative Richard Roudebush (R. Ind.) about Walker's reinstatement. In turn, Roudebush inquired about the situation to U.S. Defense Secretary Robert S. McNamara. His reply had been that since an Act had rescinded the medal in 1916, an Act would have to be initiated to restore it. He further expressed a doubt that such an action would ever happen. There were other skeptics at the highest levels. But the grassroots campaign continued.

Then it happened.

A letter from the U.S. Senate Veterans Affairs Committee, dated November 25, 1974, was sent to Ann Walker. It read, in part, "It's clear your great-grandaunt was not only courageous during the term she served as a contract doctor in the Union Army, but also as an out spoken proponent of feminine rights. Both as a doctor and feminist, she was much ahead of her time and as is usual, she was not regarded kindly by many of her contemporaries. Today she appears prophetic."

After over sixteen years, Ann Walker's campaign was gaining attention. The Army Board of Military Records agreed to a review. That was the beginning of consideration for restoration. The process moved slowly. Ann Walker was seventy-four years old.

Finally, a bill to restore the Medal of Honor to Dr. Mary E. Walker was being sent to the U.S. Congress for their consideration.

In 1977, Senator Les Aspen, a Wisconsin Democrat in the House of Representatives introduced a measure to restore the

Medal of Honor to Mary Walker. In the Senate, Edward W. Brooke, a Republican from Massachusetts, and Birch Bayh, a Democrat, from Indiana, co-sponsored a similar resolution.

Consideration eventually came to the Correction of Military Records office which recommended to Secretary of the Army, Clifford Alexander that the medal be restored. They found that the 1916 Board may have errored.

On June 10, 1977, Alexander fully restored official recognition. Next, it went to President Jimmy Carter's desk to be signed.

President Carter was put under a great deal of pressure from many women's organizations, and perhaps even his own wife and mother to restore the honor. He did so on June 11, 1977.

A spokesperson at the Carter Presidential Library in tlanta said the President "had thought it was the right thing to do."

Hurray! Ann Wilson and thousands of women and men across the United States had achieved a small victory. They had restored an honor to an honorable woman who had helped achieve a dream and paved the way for other women to follow.

Memorials to
Mary Edwards Walker

Sculpture of Mary Walker by Sharon Bumann erected on grounds of Oswego County Historical Museum, Oswego, New York.

U.S. Postal Service in 1982 issued a twenty-five cent postage stamp bearing portrait of Mary Walker.

SS Mary Walker, World War II Liberty Ship EC2 standard type commissioned October 30, 1943. Sold in private sale in 1963 for scrap metal.

Photographic wall display, Medal of Honor Museum. A similar recognition anticipated for new Medal of Honor Museum under construction in Arlington, Texas.

Various youth corps and women's auxiliary organizations in United States are named Mary Walker posts.

Resources

Altman, Frances, The Lady Wore Pants, *Dayton Leisure, Dayton)DailyNews,* January 19, 1967

Blankenship, H.N., *Personal Recollections of the War of the Rebellion,* Literary Digest Vol.IV (1912) March 15, 1919

Booth, Glenda C., "D.C. Sisters that Recall Suffragists." Baltimore Beacon, December 2020, p.34.

Chaker, Anna Marie."It's Salad Days for Weeds," The Wall Street Journal, May 27, 2009

Clark, Denise M. Dr. Mary Walker The Lady Wore Pants, History's Women's Online Magazine, 2000

Cleveland, Grover. An article, *Ladies Home Journal,* May 1905

Cole, Ben. Top U.S. Medal Figures in Plea, The Indianapolis Star, June 11, 1961 P.18,Sec. 1

Denyett, Andrea Stulman. *"Weird and Wonderful: The Dime Museum of America,"* New York University Press, 1966, New York.

Desfor, Irving. Civil War Photo Display Honors Matthew Brady, AP Features, The Tulsa Tribune, March 5, 1961

Durant, John and Allice, *Pictorial History of American Presidents.* A.S. Barnes & Company

Gerber, Sophia P, *World's Largest Wheel,* published by National Research Bureau, 1965

George Getze, Profiles in Science: Elizabeth Blackwell. Times Mirror Syndicate, Los Angeles, CA. 1961

Graf, Mercedes. *Introduction to "Hit" Essays on Women's Rights* by Mary E. Walker (1971 edition) Reprint

Graf, Mercedes, *"A Woman of Honor, Dr. Mary Walker and the Civil War."* Thomas Publications, 2001, Gettsburg, PA.

Groves, Ernest R., *An American Woman,* Emerson Books, Inc., New York, 1944.

Hugill, P.J., *World Trade,* John Hopkins University Press, p, 128.

Hutchins, Alma R., *A Handbook of Native American Herbs,* Shambhala Press, Boulder, Colorado, 1992.

Kaminski, Thereca. *"Dr. Mary Walker's Civil War and one woman's journey to the Medal of Honor and the fight for women's rights."* Lyon's Press, Guiford, Connecticut, 2021

Knauff, Margie, *"The Move Toward Rational Dress,"* " The National Dress Movement" Essay April 27, 2004.

Lewis, Ethel, *The White House.* Dodd, Mead & Co. Chapter XV, p.202.

Lockwood, Allison, "Pantsuited Pioneer of Women's Lib, Dr. Mary Walker." Smithsonian Magazine, March, 1977.

Slater, Leonard, *Woman's Suffrage*, McCalls Magazine, Vol. LXXXVIII No. 12, September 1961

Spiegel, Allen D. and Andrea M. Spiegel. *Civil War Doctoress Mary : Only Woman to Win the Congressional Medal of Honor,* Minerva: Quarterly Report on Women in Military 12, No,. 3 (1994):24

Thall, J. R. "Natural Hygiene" talk reprinted by Smithsonian Institute, Chapter XXX, December 20, 2004.

Thomas, Martha. *Amazing Mary* in *Civil War Times Illustrated* 23, No. 1 (1984):36-41 Amazing Mary

Tousignant, Marylou, *Six Military Women and Six U.S. Wars, The Washington Post* , October 18, 1997, page A13.

Parker, Sandra V. *"Richmond's Civil War Prisons"* H.H. Howard c.1990

Price, Angel. Article "Walt Whitman's Drum Taps and Washington's Civil War Hospitals"

Skiner, C. Douglas. *"Medal of Honor 1865 to Present,* " Home of Heroes.com website 1999-2009, Pueblo, Colorado.

Spiegel, Allen D., and Andrea M. *Spiegel "Civil War Doctoress Mary: Only Woman to Win Congressional Medal of Honor,"* Minerva: Quarterly Report on Women in Military 12, No.3 (1994);24

Terwillinger, Cate. *Changing the Face of Courage: Author Wants Women to See Their Strengths, The Denver Post*, May 14, 2000.

Thomas, Martha. "Amazing Mary," Civil War Times Illustrated 23, No.1 (1984):36-41

Vanden Brock, Tom. *Only One Medal of Honor given in Conflicts in Iraq, Afghanistan*, December 28, 2005, *USA Today* p. 6A

Walker, Dale L. *"Mary Edwards Walker, Above and Beyond."* Tom Boherty Associates, Book, New York.

Walker, Mary Edwards. *"Unmasked, or The Science of Immortality: to gentle-men,"* by A Woman Physician and Surgeon. Wm. H. Boyd, 717 Samson St . 1878. Available in Hathi: Trust Digital Library, Duke University.

Williams, Rudi. *Only Woman Medal of Honor Holder Ahead of Her Time,* American Services Press Service, *History's Women Online Magazine* 2000

Wilmore, Kathy. *Dr. Mary Walker's War: An American History Play, Scholastic,* Inc. 1996-2003 teacher.scholastic.com

Wood, J.D., "Disability History Museum." Reprinted in Atlantic Monthly, June 1985

Woodward, Helen Beal, *The Bold Women*, Farrer, Straus & Young, 1953

Collections

Congressional Medal of Honor, Archives and Research, website: cmohs.org

Hygiene Library Catalog, "Convalescence Natural Hygiene, Chapter XXX

Hathi: Trust Digital Library , Duke University "Unmasked."

History of Medicine Collection, (Duke University) NcD Philadelphia W.H. Boyd 1878

Lida Poynter Collection, Drexel University Archives and Special Collections, College of Medicine and Homeopathy (London visit and Letters.)

Universelle Exposition of 1867, Reprints *World's Fair* Magazine, Wikipedia

Mary Edwards Walker papers, Special Collection Research Center, Syracuse University Library, New York

Index

Acknowledgments

An author does not write a book alone. Many people, historical references and resources contribute. Thank you to George Demass, Historian, Oswego Town Hall Historical Museum, and my editorial support, author Flo McCahon and Samantha Dickson of Apprentice Press. Many telephone calls and letters were responded to by staffers at U.S. Army Women's Museum, Office of the Deputy Postmaster General, U.S. Post Office Department Library, Department of U.S. Army Office of Adjenct General for Information. And to the late Mercedes Graf who introduced me to this book's subject.

About the Author

This is the fifth biography by the author who spent over twenty years researching the subject. Writing is both Altman's career tool and hobby. She began writing children's stories and books as a stay-at- home mother. Then moved into news writing with Field Enterprises' community papers and *The Chicago Sun Times*. Later she took positions with Teepak, National Sausage Council, Allied Signal and Virginia Commonwealth University, also teaching there. Simultaneously she obtained a Masters MS degree from Roosevelt University.

Altman's subject matter has varied, from business communications to news reporting and historical commentary. Her work has received awards from National Federation of Press Women, National League of American Pen Women, Public Relations Society of America, and Northern Illinois library Assn. She also received a TWIN award from the national YWCA for her leadership, and work with nonprofit organizations.

Apprentice
House Press
Loyola University Maryland

Apprentice House is the country's only campus-based, student-staffed book publishing company. Directed by professors and industry professionals, it is a nonprofit activity of the Communication Department at Loyola University Maryland.

Using state-of-the-art technology and an experiential learning model of education, Apprentice House publishes books in untraditional ways. This dual responsibility as publishers and educators creates an unprecedented collaborative environment among faculty and students, while teaching tomorrow's editors, designers, and marketers.

Eclectic and provocative, Apprentice House titles intend to entertain as well as spark dialogue on a variety of topics. Financial contributions to sustain the press's work are welcomed. Contributions are tax deductible to the fullest extent allowed by the IRS.

To learn more about Apprentice House books or to obtain submission guidelines, please visit www.apprenticehouse.com.

Apprentice House
Communication Department
Loyola University Maryland
4501 N. Charles Street
Baltimore, MD 21210
Ph: 410-617-5265
info@apprenticehouse.com • www.apprenticehouse.com

CPSIA information can be obtained
at www.ICGtesting.com
Printed in the USA
JSHW012234160423
40386JS00001B/5